JOURNALISM
THAT
MATTERS

JOURNALISM THAT MATTERS

How Business-to-Business Editors
Change the Industries They Cover

Edited by Robert Freedman and Steven Roll

Marion Street Press, Inc.
Oak Park, Illinois

Cover design by Isabella Mathews.
Interior design assistance by Julie Fournier.

ISBN 1-933338-08-3
Printed in U.S.A.
Printing 10 9 8 7 6 5 4 3 2 1

Marion Street Press, Inc.
PO Box 2249
Oak Park, IL 60303
866-443-7987
www.marionstreetpress.com

On the Cover

U.S. Rep. Curt Weldon (R-Pa.), with a copy of the inaugural issue of *HSToday* at a Capitol Hill press conference, calling for increased funding for emergency trauma care centers. Photo reproduced with permission of *HSToday*. Photo: Tom Williams.

Table of Contents

JOURNALISM
THAT
MATTERS

Foreword

I don't remember the exact context in which I brought up the subject. It was during a Missouri School of Journalism general faculty meeting, and I spoke about the business-to-business press and the kind of excellent reporting I had seen done in its publications.

A colleague, a prize-winning journalist herself, immediately challenged me: "You are not trying to say that those kinds of magazines practice legitimate journalism, are you?"

The perception that the trade press (and I am afraid that many still use that word pejoratively) serves as nothing more than a public-relations instrument for the industry that it serves is difficult, if not impossible, to change, even among so-called objective journalists. Perhaps, as matter of fact, they are the most biased.

Granted, a publication serves its industry best when it serves its members. But it does that only by hard, straight, no-nonsense reporting—often by some of the best investigative work done anywhere. It's not surprising that the daily press often has to catch up to what the trade press has uncovered.

This book represents what is best about the trade press and the people in it. It should not only dispel some of the ridiculous notions of what the press at its best does, but it should also serve as an inspiration to those working inside and outside this vital and important facet of journalism. It may even wake up some journalism professors to inspire young students to join it.

Don Ranly, Ph.D.
Professor Emeritus
Missouri School of Journalism

Note From ASBPE

Just when did business-to-business publications become a vital part of journalism?

The truth, of course, is that "the trades" have always provided irreplaceable links within their industries or business fields. And the mainstream press long has cherry-picked information from business-to-business publications—sometimes with attribution and sometimes without—when a gem was perceived as serving a wider audience. In the 23 years I covered metals, and later defense, for *The Wall Street Journal*, I routinely drew on material I read in metals-industry and aerospace trades that I couldn't find elsewhere.

But as the case studies in this book suggest, much has changed in recent years. Today, trade publications make waves in the business world with much greater frequency than before. My own employer of the past ten years, *CFO*, a magazine for corporate finance professionals published by The Economist Group, prides itself on making waves. Our annual national state-tax survey is a good example. It's circulated well beyond our normal finance-executive and CEO audiences because industry leaders make key decisions based on our data.

The national editorial excellence awards hosted by the American Society of Business Publication Editors, known as the Azbees, have tracked this revolution. Each year the group honors ever more dramatic, ever more significant news-breaking stories. Our Stephen Barr Feature-Writing Award recently recognized coverage of China's scrap industry that became major *New York Times* news a few months after it ran in *Scrap* magazine. In fact, the same writer produced both stories.

B2B journalists are proud to occupy this significant corner of the press. This book shows why they are.

Roy Harris
President
American Society of Business Publication Editors

Note From TABPI

Two years ago, my niece was at a college recruitment fair and she told a journalism professor of her interest in the trade press. The professor's response was telling: "What, do you want to end up writing about concrete?"

The chapters in this long-overdue book reveal one of the best kept secrets in journalism: business-to-business (or "trade") publication editors play a crucial role in reporting on, acting as agents of change for, and making a difference in, the industries they cover, industries as diverse as accounting, food service, sales, and, yes, even concrete.

Editors working in the B2B press should read this book to see what the best publications are doing for their industries. Students considering a career in journalism—as well as journalism professors—would do well to study these case histories to see what kind of difference B2B editors are making.

Paul Heney
President
Trade, Association and Business Publications International

About the American Society of Business Publication Editors (ASBPE) and Trade, Association, and Business Publications International (TABPI)

All of the contributors to this volume and the publications they work for are either members of, or have had their work recognized by, these two organizations for business publication editors.

ASBPE was founded in 1964 to promote best practices in trade publication editing and to recognize outstanding work in the field. The organization's awards competition has grown considerably since its founding and now typically attracts more than 2,500 entries a year, organized under some 30 editorial, design, and Web categories. The group, with a membership of about 750, hosts editorial conferences and workshops at the national, regional, and local levels. The group also conducts industry research, including a regular compensation and job satisfaction survey, and maintains a regularly updated code of ethics. The group maintains a Web site at www.asbpe.org.

TABPI was launched in 2004 to host an international competition among editors of English-language trade publications. The competition attracted almost 700 entries in 2005 from publications in Australia, Canada, China, India, New Zealand, Singapore, South Africa, the U.K., and the U.S., among others, and was on track to grow submissions beyond that in 2006. TABPI maintains a Web site at www.tabpi.org.

JOURNALISM
THAT
MATTERS

Chapter 1

Editors as Change-makers

When I first came to Washington, D.C., in 1989 I landed a job at an obscure publication called *Housing & Development Reporter* that covered government housing programs. It didn't strike me as an exciting beat but since I had little journalism background—only a short stint at a small community newspaper in northern Nevada—I was grateful for the chance to be covering anything in the Capitol.

I was also looking forward to the possibility of making a difference.

Only a few months before I had taken the job, the main federal agency that I was preparing to cover was all over the news. The U.S. Department of Housing and Urban Development had been the front-page story in *The New York Times*, *The Washington Post*, and all the other major consumer media because of an influence-peddling scandal.

James Watt, the secretary of interior in Ronald Reagan's administration who became infamous for his attempts to open federal lands to commercial interests, had found lucrative work lobbying HUD on behalf of developers after leaving his administration post.

The result of all the media attention on his and others' activities at HUD was a raft of investigations, including one of the longest-running independent counsel investigations ever mounted, that eventually led to major HUD reform legislation when Jack Kemp was the department secretary.

It was exciting for me to cover the reform effort. But what was more satisfying was knowing that what launched this massive clean-up effort was a fellow trade journalist.

Andre Shashaty was a writer who had spent time at *Housing &*

Development Reporter and other housing trade publications and had written a piece for a tabloid called *Multi-Housing News* in which he provided the first report of the influence peddling that was going on at HUD.

His piece, based on information he had compiled from weeks of sifting through records in the bowels of the department, appeared in September 1988 and, as you would expect, its release hardly made a blip outside the industry.

But it did have one effect. When a HUD Inspector General report was issued about six months later that touched on the issues Andre uncovered, the press did something it hadn't done before: it took notice of what the HUD IG said. And the rest, as they say, is history.

Andre went on to launch his own housing trade magazine and then his own publishing company, which I joined in the late 1990s. But he never lost his appetite for entrepreneurial reporting, and my appreciation for the kind of work that trade journalists do has grown over the years as my own involvement in the business has deepened.

It's true the consumer press gets all the glory. People remember Gwen Ifill's coverage of the HUD scandal for *The Washington Post*, and rightly so, because it was solid work. But only housing industry veterans remember that Andre broke the story.

The fact is, the kind of work Andre did on that piece goes on every day in the trade press, but by its nature, the trade press flies under the radar screen of the general public.

That's not to say there's no intersection between the trade press and consumer media. Editors of consumer publications routinely ply the trade press for story ideas and to get news leads. Bryan Gruley, a senior editor in the Washington bureau for *The Wall Street Journal*, used to rely heavily on *Communications News* when he was covering telecommunications for the *Journal*.

Gruley and other consumer publication editors who sat on a panel with me a few years ago at the National Press Club extolled the trade press for giving them the background they need for the issues they don't cover every day. Indeed, hardly a week goes by without *The Washington Post* or *The New York Times* reporting on, or seeking context from, something that first came up in the trade press, like *The Washington Post* editorial that ran the day after the Sago disaster in January 2006, which left 12 miners dead. Sago's safety record had been no mystery to *Mine Safety and Health News*. That trade publication had reported that the company's accident rate was three times the national average in 2004. Maybe if that news had gotten into the right hands in

2005, the accident never would have occurred.

Fortunately, important work by the trade press doesn't need to get picked up by the editors of *The New York Times* to have an impact. As the pieces in this book show, the work of trade journalists is making a difference whether or not the national media spotlight is shining; like when John Gannon of the Bureau of National Affairs exposed the unconscionable weaknesses of the U.S. Occupational Safety and Health Administration's material safety data sheets in BNA's *Daily Report for Executives* and later in its *Right-to-Know Planning Guide.*

These data sheets are like the nutrition labels on food products, except they're for industrial chemicals. Among other things, they're supposed to instruct people handling the chemicals how to avoid volatile interactions with other substances. But in reviewing reports by a federal chemical safety board, it became clear to Gannon that the data sheets were often inaccurate and that some industrial accidents could be traced in part to these bad data sheets. Yet the federal government was doing little to address the problem—until Gannon's coverage helped spur it to action.

"For two months, I did not get a solid answer to a single question" from OSHA, says Gannon, but after his article came out, a worker-safety advocate "called and offered to help in any way he could. He started by writing to Secretary of Labor Elaine Chao, asking for her assistance in resolving the problems and enclosing a copy of the story…. Chao responded with a one-page letter indicating that she had asked OSHA Assistant Secretary John Henshaw to review the agency's data sheets policies to see whether changes were warranted." Months later, Gannon says, Henshaw had completed the review "and offered an initiative to improve data sheet accuracy."

Spurring public and private entities to action is what the pieces in this compilation are all about. Each in its own way represents a driving force in the industry it covers. For Gannon's piece, it's the industrial chemical industry; for a piece by Frank Tiboni, formerly of *Federal Computer Week,* it's the federal information technology industry. Tiboni broke a story that China had infiltrated certain U.S. Army computer networks and was gathering a treasure trove of data on Army logistics. *The Washington Post* and *The New York Times* as well as the big broadcast media picked up on Tiboni's story and the resulting publicity helped push the U.S. Department of Defense to speed its network fixes.

What the pieces in this compilation make clear is that solid reporting and the publicity it generates is *the* formula for driving industry change. A piece by Alice Lipowicz in IT trade magazine *Washington Technology* is a case in point. Lipowicz covered a session at a trade show at which the launch of a new public-private advisory board for federal information security professionals was announced. At the launch, analysts and others expressed concern over the board structure, in particular an intention to charge a limited number of companies $75,000 to become sponsoring members, which would win them a seat at the board meetings. Lipowicz's ongoing coverage of the criticism and the response to the critics by the board's supporters, posted in installments on the publication's Web site, created a feedback loop that, in only nine days, led to collapse of the plan.

A sister publication to *Washington Technology* called *Government Computer News* provoked similar change when it posted a news story on its Web site revealing that a high-level IT official in the U.S. Department of Homeland Security had burnished her credentials with a Ph.D. she had bought from a diploma mill. Within days of *GCN*'s coverage the official had been suspended, the story was all over the news, and Congress was preparing for hearings that eventually led to changes at the U.S. Office of Personnel Management in how federal agencies were to handle academic claims on job applications.

By coincidence, the examples I've noted so far involve Washington-based publications, but as you'll see in the pieces we've compiled here, industry-changing coverage is being done in publications throughout the country and even outside it.

In a hugely entertaining piece, Matthew Rushton writes about an article he wrote for London-based *Legal Business* in which he surveyed the attitudes of attorneys on the judges who sit on the Technology and Construction Court in the United Kingdom. That court hears some of the most important cases in the U.K., yet there's been smoldering dissatisfaction in the legal community with many of the judges. What Rushton's piece did was unheard of. It broke down the wall of tradition that for generations stifled criticism of judges except in cloakrooms and pubs. When the piece came out at the end of 2004, it came to the attention of the Lord Chief Justice of England and Wales, and the result was a court shake-up that led to the retirement of one of the judges and a move to reform how the court operates.

As Rushton says at the close of his essay for this book, it was "job done" for a publication that had hoped to see the court opened up a bit.

Not all of the changes that the publications drive are quite so weighty. Jenny Adams, associate editor of *Nightclub & Bar* magazine in Oxford, Miss., set out to write a profile of a club that was trying to go against type in Destin, Fla. Conventional wisdom said the area was a T-shirts and sandals kind of place, but the new club, called Rockstar Destin, placed a bet that it could get people to dress up for a night of New York-style dancing. The bet paid off, with some help from the magazine's in-depth reporting on the concept, and the ensuing interest the piece generated from others in the industry won the club's 28-year-old owner a place at the industry's big trade show to bring his formula for success to others.

Journalism with results is the currency of business-to-business publications. It would take some legwork but it wouldn't be hard to fill this volume with a hundred examples of pieces that have made a difference. What we've done instead is showcase a representative sample of change-making work. To capture what we think is a good balance, we include pieces from traditional trade magazines like *Nightclub & Bar*, tabloids like *Government Computer News*, newsletters like *Transfer Pricing Report*, association publications like *ABA Child Law Practice*, peer-reviewed journals like the *Journal of Government Financial Management*, and publications that sit in the nexus between trade and the consumer publications like *PC World*.

We know there are great stories out there that aren't included here, but this sample gives us the basis for distilling a few rules for driving change-making journalism. Steven Roll, editor of *State Tax Law Report* and co-editor of this volume, outlines those rules in his piece, "How Editors Push Industries Forward."

For editors, these rules should be useful as you approach your own industry coverage. Is there a smoldering issue in your industry that people talk about but on which action is never taken? Hard-hitting coverage by your publication might be the boost that's needed to break through the inertia to get your industry's agents of change moving.

For journalism students, the rules and the essays will give you an inside look at what editors and writers face when they're confronting challenging coverage questions.

What's more, we think you'll find the essays a great read. In concise language, the writers walk you through the events that led to their coverage, the challenges they confronted, and the outcomes their pieces produced. We also include a reprint of the subject article and a short information box on the publication. Taken together, the pieces should give you a picture of solid trade journalism at work—and, we hope, help you as you carry on your own important work.

—*Robert Freedman*

JOURNALISM
THAT
MATTERS

Chapter 2

How Editors Push
Industries Forward

As I lifelong fan of *All the President's Men*, I can tell you that the recipe for producing change-making journalism is not transferred through osmosis. For as much as I was thrilled by Bob Woodward and Carl Bernstein's story, I've yet to replicate their success in uncovering malfeasance, maybe because I haven't been able to find my own "Deep Throat" to lead me through a Byzantine scandal within the field I cover: state taxation.

But some of my colleagues in the business press have. And as you'll see from the pieces collected in this volume, they know how to produce high-impact stories, sometimes with the help of their own Deep Throat. But they, too, might be hard-pressed to articulate a recipe for success for others to follow.

To be sure, the factors for success that prize-winning B2B journalists often cite such as "hard work" or "cultivating sources" ring true at the awards podium. But after we give them our polite applause, we know these nostrums provide little insight as we seek to produce the same level of quality in our work.

That said, an analysis of the business press pieces compiled in this book yields several things we can learn from our colleagues.

In the Beginning is a Gap

To begin with, although the range of subject matter of the pieces is extremely broad—they range from government computer hacking to sloppy beach wear—the lion's share of pieces revolve around a gap between perception and reality. In some cases the gap is made apparent by a tipster who comes to us with a juicy tidbit. You'll see that in the pieces in *Government Computer News* and *Housing Affairs Letter*. To this day, only the editors of *GCN* know who provided the tip that a high-ranking official at the U.S. Department of Homeland Security received her college degrees—all three of them—from a diploma mill. Similarly, only the editors of *Housing Affairs Letter* know the identity of the person who brought a brazen lobbying scheme to their attention.

In other cases, the gap between perception and reality has been apparent to everyone for years, but no one's had the courage to say the emperor has no clothes. The piece from *The Electrical Distributor*, or *TED*, is a case in point. Everyone knew manufacturers' rebates were an albatross around the industry's neck, but it took a push by the editors of the magazine to help get reform efforts started. In still other cases, it's pure sleuthing that brings to light the perception gap. John Gannon found it intriguing that so many chemical accidents involved bad material handling data sheets, then wrote about what he learned in *Daily Report for Executives*. Frank Tiboni of *Federal Computer Week* questioned why the U.S. Army was suddenly upgrading so many of its communications systems. It turned out the upgrade was really a big patching exercise to keep out spies who had infiltrated their logistics networks.

We're From the Government and We're Here to Help

In the majority of the articles we compiled, the editors cite the need for some type of government action, a change in policy or personnel, a new regulation, or enactment of legislation. Some of these stories spur the government to act immediately, such as the *GCN* piece. Once that piece came out, the Homeland Security official was suspended within days.

A shake-up in the United Kingdom's Technology and Construction Court that was fueled by a *Legal Business* article was immediate, too. The Lord Chief Justice of England and Wales wasted no time sacking a judge and ordering reform once it was clear that disgruntlement with the court among attorneys exposed by the piece was true.

Others produce change over time. A series of pieces by *Professionally Speaking*, a Toronto-based magazine for teachers, helped persuade provincial lawmakers to make a huge investment in teacher training, but it took years to accomplish.

In some cases, the reform process is still on-going. A good example is government financial management reform, spurred in part by a provocative piece in the *Journal of Government Financial Management*. In that case, members of Congress and officials in the executive branch are tapping ideas expressed in the piece while they look at reform, but they're still far from actually implementing any of the ideas.

A piece by Molly Moses of *Transfer Pricing Report* also helped spark efforts at reform, in this case between tax authorities in the U.S. and Canadian governments. Here again reform is moving slowly, but it's unlikely it would be moving at all if Moses hadn't shown just how deeply divided the two countries had become on how to tax certain companies with trans-border operations.

We're From Industry, and We Can Reform Ourselves, Thank You

The other stories spur intra-industry reform. For example, a series of articles published by *ABA Child Law Practice* persuaded over-worked, under-paid lawyers to talk about the need for professional practice standards. Once the idea gelled, the articles were used as the basis for the standards, and today lawyers are slowly but surely adopting the new practices.

The editors of *PC World* took matters into their own hands after an industry expert suggested that they verify claims computer manufacturers were making about their monitors. The magazine independently tested the monitors to see how they lined up with the specifications manufacturers touted to consumers. The article, which showed a gap between what manufacturers were saying and what the magazine's independent testing showed, caused an industry committee to discuss more rigorous testing standards.

Efforts by *Engineering News Record* had a similar impact. Industry experts complained to the editors that project scheduling software had loopholes that let people manipulate schedules, an industry no-no to veteran schedulers. The editors aired the issue and sparked some software manufacturers to close the loophole.

Exchange of Best Practices

Just as important as reform is the role B2B editing plays in the exchange of best practices that industries rely on to speed progress. There's probably nothing that B2B publications do better. The piece in *Security Management* is a good example. In it, an industry expert shows how he improved site security while squeezing efficiency out of his security budget by requiring a contractor to have a financial stake in its performance. The article motivated another security executive to try the practice at his own company, and in that way best practices are born.

The editors of *Nightclub & Bar* furthered their industry's best practices in much the same way when it ran a profile of a new nightclub in Florida that eschewed the typical beach-party atmosphere that appealed to the T-shirt-and-sandals set in favor of a more formal New York City dance scene.

In light of what we found in looking at our selection of articles, here are seven things to look for as you plan your publication's coverage going forward:

■ A controversial government policy or practice

■ A problem that the government has ignored or failed to address adequately

■ An industry practice that is widely accepted, but needing reform

■ Practical guidelines to improve performance within the industry

■ An analysis of suspect claims made by members of an industry

■ A report that draws on the general consensus of what industry members think about a sensitive matter within the field

■ A novel or unique approach to doing business

The qualities that separate a solidly reported article from one that has a lasting impact on a government or industry are hard to pin down. But the case studies in this book show us that there are a variety of ways to go about producing high-impact business press stories. Focusing on what these B2B editors did right offers an inspiring and valuable lesson.

—Steven Roll

Making a Difference: Patterns in Trade Editorial Practice

There's no formula for developing hard-hitting B2B publication pieces that lead to concrete industry change, but a look at the articles compiled in this book show that change-making trade journalism unfolds in just a few different ways. Although anonymous tips probably make the best cocktail party conversation, unknown sources as the driving force behind a piece are the exception, not the rule; in most pieces, the editor is aware of longstanding problems in an industry and by simply adopting the issue as a cause, industry leaders are spurred to action. In other cases, editors come across something that doesn't look right and, through their initiative, uncover a problem. In the table on the following pages, "Approach" refers to the chief way the editor gathered information for the piece or pieces that led to action on the problem.

Publication	Problem	Source	Approach	Result
Federal Computer Week	Unsecured network	Editor initiative	Interviews	Repairs hastened
Daily Report for Executives	Inaccurate chemical handling instructions	Editor initiative	Interviews	Reforms introduced
Legal Business	Unhappy attorneys	Editor initiative	Survey	Reforms launched
Engineering News-Record	Software loophole	Disgruntled experts	Interviews	Loopholes closed
Housing Affairs Letter	Potential conflict of interest	Anonymous letter	Interviews	Conflict averted
Government Computer News	Credential inflation	Anonymous letter	Analyses	Verification process launched
Transfer Pricing Report	Tax dispute	Widely known	Interviews	Resolution discussed
Washington Technology	Potential conflict of interest	Widely known	Interviews	Conflict averted
The Electrical Distributor	Inefficient pricing	Industry expert	Opinion pieces, analyses	Reforms launched
Journal of Government Financial Management	Inefficient rules	Industry expert	Opinion piece	Reforms discussed

Publication	Problem	Source	Approach	Result
HSToday	Inadequate facilities funding	Widely known	Interviews	Reforms discussed
Professionally Speaking	Inadequate education funding	Industry expert	Opinion pieces, analyses	Funding increased
PC World	Inaccurate specifications	Industry expert	Testing	Reforms discussed
ABA Child Law Practice	Inadequate representation	Industry expert	Opinion pieces, analyses	Standards implemented
Security Management	Contractor inefficiency	Industry expert	Case study	Best practice shared
Public Power	Inefficient pricing	Industry experts	Opinion pieces, analyses	Reforms discussed
Nightclub & Bar	Old business model	Widely known	Profile	Best practice

JOURNALISM
THAT
MATTERS

Chapter 3

Getting Real on Virtual Espionage

Spurred by Federal Computer Week, *the U.S. Department of Defense acknowledges weaknesses in its computer network*

In the world of espionage, a U.S. intelligence case officer recruits an agent and the two secretly swap information. The exchange, usually at a meeting, is the most risky part of the relationship and typically where the two get caught. But what if a case officer could bypass the exchange and still get the info he wants?

China has perfected this form of spying using computer espionage. Since 2003, Chinese hackers have obtained U.S. military secrets, including how U.S. military generals will command their forces on the battlefield in the future, by breaking into U.S. Department of Defense computer networks. They find holes in hardware and software that get them into DOD networks, they search until they locate what they want, and they install cyber Trojan horses—malicious computer code—that corrupts data, slows networks, and allows them to come and go as they please.

The U.S. military has given the codename "Titan Rain" to China's hacking of its networks. I broke this computer security story in a two-part series called "The New Trojan War." The August 2005 series, which received widespread attention in the national news media, culminated an investigation I had begun two years earlier. I interviewed U.S. military and government leaders, and met with, and obtained DOD documents from, information technology industry officials who were troubled with the U.S. military's slow response to secure its networks.

The story is very important to U.S. national security. From a philosophical perspective, DOD is moving toward a strategy of network-centric warfare. The department believes rapidly making available information to fighters anywhere in the world is the key to winning the war on terrorism. But what good is information if you can't protect it and the enemy has a bead on your movements? From an operational viewpoint, China is becoming an economic and military superpower. China wants to reclaim Taiwan. The United States has pledged to defend the democratic country. This means the two countries could find themselves at war in the future, and information China obtains on how the U.S. military will fight that war could give them an advantage.

I started investigating Titan Rain for the publication I wrote for at the time, *Federal Computer Week*, in the fall of 2003, after Army plans to upgrade communications systems and better protect computer networks six months into the war in Iraq made me curious. The reason for the upgrade, they said, was to treat all communications systems as part of a cohesive enterprise. But I was skeptical. Why were so many communications and computer security plans going on at once? I put the question to IT industry officials who worked for the Army. I said something bad must have happened. The Army, like most government agencies, is reactive instead of proactive.

Although some IT industry officials talked, most didn't. The ones that did requested and received anonymity. They confirmed my hunch. They told me that Army networks, especially at Fort Campbell, Ky., the home of the service's elite attack helicopter units, were under attack from China and the service was doing little about it.

The story was sensational: China, an emerging superpower, in a cyber war with the United States, the lone superpower, while it wages

Federal Computer Week
Smart Government Starts Here

Federal Computer Week

www.fcw.com

Established: 1987

Publisher: FCW Media Group, Falls Church, Va.

Frequency: 42 issues per year

Characteristics: Four-color magazine

Circulation: 101,329

Readership: Federal information technology managers

Editorial staff: 24 editors, writers, designers

the war on terrorism.

I went to my editor with the scoop. He liked the story. But he refused to publish it at first because the information came from IT industry officials who could profit from the story. He told me to corroborate it.

In early June 2004, I got my first break at an Army computer conference in Hershey, Pa. At breakfast on the last day of the show, when most journalists and attendees had already left, I randomly sat at a table with several IT industry officials. I started chatting with them. They were employed by a company that worked on Army computer security. I asked them about the hackings at Fort Campbell and they confirmed them. They told me the Army was also readying a plan to fortify its networks.

In July 2004, I reported in a story that the Army planned to spend millions of dollars in early 2005 to strengthen networks in a project called the secure server initiative. I also wrote that hackers attacked them at an important U.S. military installation in August 2003 and January 2004. My editor chose to leave out Fort Campbell until we could get more information. He felt we needed an Army document or an Army admission confirming the attacks.

After that story was published, I continued pursuing the story. I talked more with the IT industry officials I met at the conference. I also spoke again with the IT industry officials with whom I had first discussed the story. I also interviewed Army IT and military officials and Army IT workers at Fort Campbell. They requested questions via e-mail. I obliged and waited for the responses. I was then passed around Army agencies to get my questions answered, which was frustrating. They took six weeks to respond. The answers I received were the same comments I would get for the next year. "We are a nation at war, and although protection of our networks has always had a high priority, we are even more vigilant now. The less the enemy knows, the better it is for the people [who] protect our networks. I will not go into specifics on what types of defensive measures we have in place. However, I will say that great emphasis is placed on constant vigilance."

In September 2004, I wrote my first major story on Titan Rain, "Army rebuilds networks after hack attacks." I reported that a Chinese hacker had broken into an administrative network at Fort Campbell and was in it for three months before the service noticed. To cleanse and secure networks there, I wrote, the Army spent $30 million in a program it called the Fort Campbell network upgrade. Although I reported that a Chinese hacker was in a network there, I did not say that the Chinese government was behind it. Again, my editor was not comfortable reporting that given the information I had. "Get a military document or a current or former military official saying it and then I'll think about it," he said.

I continued talking and meeting with my sources. I pushed them to get me a U.S. military document citing China or to put me in touch with a U.S. military official. I developed a new industry source, one that eventually agreed to help me after months of trying to convince him. The industry official requested and received anonymity and became my best source. We met every couple months for breakfast. In the meantime, DOD was taking steps to better protect its networks. In fall 2004, it issued new information assurance policies. In winter 2005, the Air Force took steps to better protect its networks. The DOD document and the Air Force initiative gave credence to my suspicion that not just Army but U.S. military networks were under attack from China.

My editor's strategy was to publish stories when I nailed them and to chip away at the larger story: China hacking DOD networks. My second break came at an Army computer conference in June 2005 in Las Vegas. An Army general said during a public speech that Fort Hood, Texas, the home of the service's first digitized division, had a huge information security problem. An Army IT official said in a public presentation there that the service had to spend millions of dollars in the past two years to rebuild networks at two bases because of hackings. Fort Campbell and Fort Hood seemed the obvious places, but was there another one? Again, on the last day of the show, when most journalists and attendees had left, I fortuitously ran into a former U.S. military officer now in the IT industry who talked to me about the hackings. The IT industry official said the Army general was referring to Fort Hood and Fort Bragg, N.C., the home of the Army's elite paratroop forces, and the hackings were similar in nature. In June 2005, I wrote my second major story on Titan Rain, "Army rebuilds network defenses after hacks," that reported the hackings at the two Army bases and the service's plan to consolidate networks and improve defenses. My editor again left China out of the story.

My editor and I sat down and discussed this story when I came back to Washington, D.C. "Why did you take China out," I asked. "When are you going to get a military document or a current or former military official admitting this," he responded. I had been working this story for a year and none of my previous stories said China was behind the DOD hackings. So I gave myself a two-month deadline to finally get the story. I focused on getting the U.S. military document or confirmation from an official.

My work paid off. I obtained two documents, one from the Army labeled "For Official Use Only," which means it is unclassified but not for public viewing, and a second from the Defense Information Systems Agency (DISA), which helps monitor U.S. military computer security, labeled unclassified. Both documents were given to me by industry officials at breakfast meetings I had set up. The source for the Army document worked closely with that branch of the military; the source for the second worked closely with DISA. Had I known about these documents before I'd been given them, I probably could have gotten them myself through a Freedom of Information Act (FOIA) request, since they were unclassified, but the process would have been drawn out—probably six months at least.

The Army document appeared to show that hackings on its networks increased from September 2003 to May 2004, spiking in March 2004, the time of Taiwan's general elections. The DISA document, which the agency said was for training, showed a world map and a line connecting Washington, D.C., and Hong Kong. My IT industry official sources said these two documents corroborated that China was hacking DOD networks.

I then interviewed Army Gen. Jack Keane, the service's recently retired vice chief of staff and a highly-respected military expert. He confirmed that China had been hacking DOD networks for two years. "It's common knowledge in the Pentagon," said Keane, who said I could attribute those comments to him. The former U.S. military officer now in the IT industry had told me that a Chinese hacker broke into a test and evaluation network in 2003 at Aberdeen Proving Ground, Md., which is where the Army tests many of its weapons systems, and obtained information on a future command and control system. The Chinese hacker was in the network for eight months before the Army discovered him. I then met with my best IT industry official source again. I told him about the hackings and that I heard there was a codename given to them. He said it was called Titan Rain. I also followed up on interviews I conducted during the past two years with the White House, the U.S. Department of Homeland Security, and the FBI. I was told officials in those agencies were investigating Titan Rain. I was denied interviews with all of them. And I knew the military would give me the same answer as to whether China was hacking DOD networks. So I patiently waited for the department to get me answers on the steps it took to counter them. I was strung along for four weeks, but I obtained them.

I told my editor what I now had. "Write the story," he said.

I wanted to approach it in two parts, one on the hackings and two on what DOD was doing about them. I chose the metaphor of the Trojan horse for my story. The Greeks used a wooden Trojan horse to get inside Troy. Chinese hackers were using Trojaned-software to get into and out of DOD networks without getting caught.

I published the first part of the story, "The New Trojan War," on Aug. 22, 2005, and the second part, "DOD's 'Manhattan Project'" (because DOD officials said their effort to strengthen network defenses is similar to building the atomic bomb) on Aug. 29, 2005. We decided to keep the codename Titan Rain out of the story. Codenames are classified and we complied with DOD's request to withhold it from publication.

The first two days after the story was published were quiet. The third day, however, the "Early Bird," the Pentagon's clipping service, picked up my story. Every day, the Early Bird publishes the most interesting stories in the press and sends them to DOD policymakers and generals via e-mail. The following day, *The Washington Post* published a story about it on the front page and revealed the codename. That afternoon, a reporter for CNN's "Lou Dobb's Tonight" called and interviewed me for a story she was doing on Titan Rain for air that night. Two days later, a *Time* magazine writer, who was also working on the story, was interviewed on MSNBC and gave his take on it.

The stories impacted DOD policy. Three months later, on Nov. 29, the department held a first-ever "security stand-down" in which all personnel around the world focused on information assurance and network security. For the entire day, they learned about better protecting DOD data and systems.

The key lesson from Titan Rain is U.S. enemies, including China, know they can't take on the powerful U.S. military, tank against tank and jet fighter against jet fighter, in combat. The U.S. military is too skilled and too technologically advanced to be defeated. To even the battlefield, U.S. enemies have learned, they can disrupt, disable, or destroy U.S. military networks, which allows the lone superpower to quickly target and attack enemy forces, to rapidly generate and share intelligence information, and to swiftly order and supply troops. Hardware and software is now every bit as important as tanks and jet fighters on today's battlefield. And securing networks and information is paramount for the U.S. military retaining its superiority on future battlefields.

—*Frank Tiboni*

The New Trojan War

Defense Department finds its networks under attack from China

By Frank Tiboni

In mythology, the Greeks found an innovative way to avoid Troy's defenses. By offering the gift of a huge horse—hollowed out and filled with soldiers—the Greeks were able to bypass Troy's defenses and attack from the inside.

Today the Pentagon faces a similar situation. Adversaries have been attacking Defense Department computer networks in attempts to bypass the United States' formidable defenses and attack from the inside out.

Defense and industry officials describe DOD networks as the Achilles' heel of the powerful U.S. military. Securing military networks is even more critical in an increasingly transformed military in which information is as much a weapon as tanks and assault rifles.

DOD networks have been breached. Department officials acknowledged hackers attacked military networks almost 300 times in 2003—sometimes by cyber Trojan horses, which can operate within an organization's network. DOD officials say intrusions reduced the military's operational capabilities in 2004.

The pace of the attacks has accelerated as adversaries honed in on this perceived weakness. DOD tallied almost 75,000 incidents on department networks last year, the most ever.

Top U.S. military cyberwarriors recently said that adversaries probe DOD computers within minutes of the systems' coming online. The cyberwarriors described DOD's computer network defense strategy as a battle of attrition in which neither side has an advantage. Retired Army officers and industry officials say Chinese hackers are the primary culprits.

During the past five years, Chinese hackers have successfully probed and penetrated DOD networks. In one intrusion, they used a Trojan horse—a program containing malicious code in an e-mail or adware—to obtain data on a future Army command and control system.

DOD takes the intrusions seriously. One of the military's proposals to strengthen its networks is building fake networks, sometimes called "Honeynets," which divert attackers from critical systems.

Yet some industry officials say Chinese hackers have already obtained the technology to challenge the U.S. military and its evolving network-centric warfare strategy, which connects systems to send information to warfighters faster.

Many Networks

DOD operates 3.5 million PCs and 100,000 local-area networks at 1,500 sites in 65 countries, and it runs thousands of applications on 35 major voice, video and data networks, including the Non-Classified IP Router Network, which is connected to the Internet, and the Secret IP Router Network, which is not.

The networks provide combat information to civilians, warfighters and analysts in support of warfare roles, but the networks represent a key vulnerability.

DOD networks were hacked 294 times in 2003, said retired Air Force Lt. Gen. Harry Raduege during an industry luncheon briefing in December 2004. He is the former commander of the Joint Task Force for Global Network Operations (JTF-GNO), the organization that operates and defends DOD networks.

Department networks remained under attack in 2004, spurring Paul Wolfowitz, the former deputy secretary of Defense, to issue a memo telling the services to redouble cybersecurity efforts.

"Recent exploits have reduced operational capabilities on our networks," he wrote in an Aug. 15, 2004, memo.

"Our adversaries are able to inflict a substantial amount of harassment and a measurable amount of damage upon DOD communications networks at practically no cost to themselves," Army Col. Carl Hunt, JTF-GNO's director of technology and analysis, co-wrote in "Net Force Maneuver: A NetOps Construct."

Hunt did not name those harassing or hacking DOD networks. However, Army officers and industry officials pointed to Chinese hackers as the primary culprits.

"The Chinese were doing this on a regular basis," said Jack Keane, the former Army vice chief of staff who retired last year. He now works as a military consultant and advises URS. "That's a given. They're very aggressively getting capability."

Keane said he received briefings on China's hacking of DOD networks. "It's common knowledge in the Pentagon," he said.

He knew of no instances in which hackers penetrated DOD networks. However, a retired Army officer who worked in information assurance remembers a hacking three years ago at Aberdeen Proving Ground, Md., where the service tests weapon systems.

The retired Army officer, who now works in systems integration in industry and requested anonymity, said a Chinese hacker used a Trojan horse to penetrate a network there and downloaded information on the capabilities of a future Army command and control system for eight months before the service detected a security breach. The system was a prototype under development testing at Aberdeen.

The retired Army officer said the Aberdeen hacking is similar to intrusions during the past three years at other Army bases. The breaches caused the service to spend tens of millions of dollars to rebuild networks. In those incidents, hackers penetrated systems at Fort Campbell, Ky., home of the 101st Airborne Division; Fort Bragg, N.C., home of the 82nd Airborne Division; and Fort Hood, Texas, home of the 4th Infantry Division.

DOD has also said that the Chinese have targeted military networks. "Beijing has focused on building the infrastructure to develop advanced space-based command, control, communications, computers, intelligence, surveillance and reconnaissance and targeting capabilities," the Pentagon said in a report issued last month. "The People's Liberation Army has likely established information warfare units to develop viruses to attack enemy computer systems and networks, and tactics to protect friendly computer systems and networks."

Army documents on weaknesses in its computer network defenses and vulnerabilities in 10 systems include one that appears to show networks under attack by China.

Although DOD officials believe improved network management and vigilance would prevent 90 percent of hackings, 10 percent may still occur because they involve new intrusion methods.

"The threat is becoming more aggressive and sophisticated," said Army Brig. Gen. Dennis Via, deputy commander of JTF-GNO.

DOD's 'Manhattan Project'

With mission-critical networks under attack, DOD works to plug holes

By Frank Tiboni

Editor's note: This is the second in a two-part series.

Taking a page from the past and one from the future, the Defense Department is devising ways to fight a new kind of threat that requires the strategic tricks of ancient warriors and the untested tools of network-centric warfare.

Unless DOD changes how it operates and learns to defend its cyber networks, many military experts say it will not be able to wage an effective battle in the cyberwar that is emerging as the 21st century's biggest challenge.

The Pentagon is at a crossroads, said Air Force Lt. Gen. Charles Croom, the new director of the Defense Information Systems Agency and commander of the Joint Task Force for Global Network Operations (JTF-GNO). "Networks are too important to the warfighter to not have them when the warfight begins," he said.

Croom said DOD approaches computer network defense by emphasizing convenience to users, but the department's future information assurance strategy should tilt toward adding security.

"The threat is great," Croom said. "It requires constant vigilance."

Other countries—for example, China—crime gangs, and thrill-seeking hackers could steal information about U.S. military war plans and weapon systems to gain intelligence and embarrass the Pentagon. The threat has caused DOD to re-evaluate information assurance policies and acknowledge that such reviews will continue.

In the past year, DOD implemented new policies to strengthen computer network defense. In 2004, DOD created JTF-GNO to operate and defend networks that operate under Strategic Command (Stratcom).

The department also approved a new command structure that identifies four military officials who will report to Croom. The National Security Agency published a new technical architecture guiding DOD's acquisition and use of information assurance technology. DOD also issued directives on managing ports, protocols and services, and requiring periodic computer security training for all department employees.

DOD turned to procurement to support these policies and develop new kinds of defenses for cyberattacks. First, the department chose Retina from eEye Digital Security to scan computers for vulnerabilities. Then, DOD selected Hercules from Citadel to patch computers. Next, the department built a new multimillion-dollar command center to monitor global network operations and picked PestPatrol, antispyware from Computer Associates International. DOD will soon begin testing Pest Patrol before introducing it later in the year.

DOD identified nine new procurements to fill information assurance gaps and improve security analyses and responses departmentwide, said a DISA official who requested anonymity.

The procurements include:

Tier 3 Security Information Manager, a comprehensive system that tracks and analyzes data produced by scanning and sensing products.

Insider Threat, technology that prevents spies and double agents from installing malicious hardware and software.

Secret IP Network Security Enhancements, a system that strengthens protection of the U.S. military's classified network.

Honeynets, fake networks that draw adversaries away from the U.S. military's real networks, keep them occupied and collect intelligence on their attack methods.

The DISA official said the Computer Network Defense Enterprise Solutions Steering Group oversees those new procurements. It is led by Stratcom and the Office of the Assistant Secretary of Defense for Networks and Information Integration and Chief Information Officer. That office develops DOD information technology policy and administers the department's $2 billion annual budget for information assurance products and services.

Bob Lentz, director of information assurance in the DOD CIO's office, said he agrees with Croom that the department is at a crossroads as it tries to operate and defend a complex of networks known as the Global Information Grid (GIG).

"This is the equivalent of the Manhattan Project," Lentz said. "I will say we are at that level of seriousness of securing this massive network."

Every four hours, he said, the equivalent of the entire Library of Congress' archives travels on DOD networks. To wage network-centric warfare, he said, the department's 4 million users must trust the confidentiality of the information that crosses GIG and be assured of its availability.

Adversaries, however, recognize the U.S. military's dependence on networks and electronic information and the importance of sharing data—all of which are main principles of the evolving net-centric warfare strategy. Enemies view that dependency as an opportunity to challenge the most powerful fighting force in the world on an even battlefield, military experts say.

Industry officials worry that all the steps the military will take might not be enough. They argue that net-centric warfare opens the services to hidden dangers.

"We tend to assume we will have a technological edge over our adversaries," said Loren Thompson, chief operating officer at the Lexington Institute, a public-policy think tank. "That quite possibly may not happen because digital networking technology is readily available in global markets."

Alan Paller, director of research at the SANS Institute, a non-profit organization that monitors computer security, warned that U.S. warfighters are becoming dependent on IT rather than using it as an enhancer.

"The risk of losing the engagement because the systems were hacked grows explosively," Paller said. President Bush has pledged to defend Taiwan if China attacks. And DOD has said the new local warfighting strategy of China's People's Liberation Army is to use computer network operations to seize the initiative and gain electromagnetic dominance early.

Jack Keane, the retired Army vice chief of staff who is now a military consultant and advises URS Corp., a federal contractor, said the new warfighting strategies of the United States and China play off each other. He said they could collide if China attacks Taiwan to unify it with the mainland.

Paul Wolfowitz, former deputy secretary of Defense, did not name China as one of the adversaries exploiting vulnerabilities in DOD networks in a memo to agency officials and military leaders last year. But "failure to secure our networks will weaken our war fighting ability and potentially put lives at risk," he said.

JOURNALISM
THAT
MATTERS

Chapter 4

Coming Clean on
Bad Chemical Data

The U.S. Occupational Safety and Health Administration wakes up to the
dangers of sloppy chemical warnings after an investigation by
Daily Report for Executives

I can't imagine chemical accident reports ever hitting the best seller lists, but when I read a report in the fall of 2001 by a newly established federal agency, the U.S. Chemical Safety and Hazard Investigation Board, on an industrial accident at the Morton International plant in Paterson, N.J., I was hooked.

I was an editor at the Bureau of National Affairs, a specialty trade publishing company in Washington, D.C., and had just been given responsibility for a small newsletter, the *Right-to-Know Planning Guide*, which covers an area of law known as chemical right-to-know. To comply with right-to-know requirements, chemical manufacturers are supposed to provide information about the health and safety risks of their products, and also proper procedures for using them in the safest manner. I read the Chemical Safety Board's reports to get up to speed on my new beat.

The reports dealt with chemical accidents, and as horrible as those are, the Chemical Board write-ups made for good reading. They clearly explained what had gone wrong and what needed to be done to prevent more disasters from occurring.

The Chemical Safety Board, like the National Transportation Safety

BNA, Inc.

Daily Report for Executives

Daily Report for Executives

www.bna.com/products/
corplaw/der.htm

Established: 1943

Publisher: Bureau of
National Affairs,
Washington, D.C.

Frequency: Daily

Characteristics: 115 pages
average

Circulation: Not available

Readership: Government
relations executives and
others following federal
legislative, judicial and
regulatory news

Editorial staff: Managing
editor, assistant managing
editor, 3 copy editors, 10
reporters, in-house
production

Board, fulfills its mandate by investigating accidents after the fact. It has no power to issue fines or promulgate regulations. Its job is to find the causes of chemical disasters, and make its findings available to the public. The first Chemical Safety Board accident report appeared in 1998.

Five full-scale reports had been issued by the board by the time I began reading them. The sixth, on a fatal fire at a Bethlehem Steel mill in Chesterton, Ind., was published in December 2001.

As in the Morton International investigation, the board's report on the Bethlehem Steel fire noted that an inaccurate material safety data sheet had been a factor in the tragedy.

Was it simply a statistical fluke that this new agency had completed only six major accident investigations and in two cases the investigators had linked the disasters partly to faulty material safety data sheets? Or was there a larger problem?

Two out of six seemed unacceptably high. Imagine the outcry if one-third of the manuals that come with new cars contained information that would destroy the car and imperil its passengers, or if one-third of the prescription drugs were sold with directions that, if followed, would cause illness, injury, or death in the patient.

There were two major obstacles I had to overcome to research this story. The first was ignorance. I had no background in chemistry, industrial hygiene, or any related field.

BNA's librarians helped me locate some studies that had been done on material safety data sheets and the studies led to sources who, after I contacted them, patiently tutored me on the underlying issues. I called everyone who I thought could be helpful, including the authors of the studies I had read. They, in turn, pointed me to analysts and others who could shed some light on aspects of the problem. At the same time, BNA reporters and editors who knew something about related topics also were generous with their time.

The second obstacle was the Occupational Safety and Health Administration, the federal agency responsible for enforcing the data sheets' accuracy.

In January 2002, I began to direct questions to a staff person in OSHA's public affairs office. It was a terrific learning experience.

What I wanted to know was very simple: Was OSHA concerned that two out of the first six board reports had listed inaccurate material safety data sheets as part of what went wrong? Was the agency surprised? Did the agency think something needed to be done about inaccurate data sheets, and if so, what was it planning to do?

For two months, I did not get a solid answer to a single question. The person ostensibly assigned to help me would take the questions down and not call back, or not be available when I called, or say that due to a technical glitch she had not gotten my latest message. In one conversation, she insisted that she did not even know who in OSHA, if anyone, was receiving and reading the board's reports.

All the while, OSHA insisted that I had to direct all questions to public affairs and not call OSHA employees directly. When I tried anyway by leaving a message on a key employee's voice mail, I quickly got a call and a lecture from the staff person.

So I sat down and drafted an e-mail to her in which I listed all the questions that she had not answered. At the end of the message, I wrote that I thought my readers would be very interested in seeing this substantial list of all the things that she, as an OSHA representative, claimed not to know and apparently was unable to find out, and that I was planning to include the list as a sidebar that would run with my story!

The e-mail was a breakthrough. A few days later I got a call from a supervisor in OSHA public affairs saying that the staffer assigned to me had been called away on a "family emergency" with no indication when she would return.

The supervisor offered to get written answers to my questions if I would put them in writing again, and she delivered on the promise.

I did not get everything I wanted because OSHA still refused to let me interview that key employee, but at least I had the agency's side.

My first story on the data sheets appeared in the May 23, 2002, issue of the *Right-To-Know Planning Guide*. As the editor, I gave it the biggest news hole in the newsletter, a little less than 850 words.

There was more to say on the topic than my modest four-page biweekly could handle. Fortunately, I work for a publisher with products that can run longer stories.

I wrote a 1,600-word version and, over the next three weeks, six other BNA newsletters ran either the longer version or the shorter version of the story.

Meanwhile, the Chemical Safety Board published the results of its investigation of a fatal accident in March 2001 at the BP Amoco plant in Augusta, Ga. For the third time, investigators fingered an inaccurate MSDS as part of what went wrong.

The 1,600-word story attracted the attention of Toby McIntosh, managing editor of the *Daily Report for Executives*, known as DER, BNA's premier publication. The newsletter is read each morning by a Who's Who of Washington lobbyists, attorneys, lawmakers, and their aides. Toby and DER copyeditor Steve France saw the potential for a bigger and more forceful story. With their suggestions and the blessing and encouragement of my managing editor, Kevin Fetherston, I wrote the story that appears in this book.

It might have ended there if not for two developments.

Number one was the continuing work of the Chemical Safety Board. In August 2002, the board issued a report on its investigation into an explosion and fire at the Motiva Enterprises refinery in Delaware City, Del., that killed one worker, injured eight others, and emptied nearly one hundred thousand gallons of acid into the Delaware River. The board noted that the explosion occurred because workers were welding near an aboveground storage tank containing spent sulfuric acid, a combustible substance. Motiva's material safety data sheet for the acid stated "the product is not combustible."

Number two was Ron Hayes. At the suggestion of a source, I faxed a copy of the story to Hayes, who directs the FIGHT project (Families in Grief Hold Together). Since the death of his 19-year-old son in a senseless grain silo accident in 1993, Hayes has dedicated his life to worker safety.

An hour after I sent the article, Hayes called and offered to help in any way he could. He started by writing to U.S. Secretary of Labor Elaine Chao, asking for her assistance in resolving the problems with material safety data sheets and enclosing a copy of the story.

In December 2002, Chao responded to Hayes with a one-page letter indicating that she had asked OSHA Assistant Secretary John

Henshaw to review the agency's data sheets policies to see whether changes were warranted.

"The issues you raise have been of long-standing concern to OSHA and to many people who use or work with MSDSs," Chao wrote, referring to the data sheets by their acronym.

The secretary's letter was the first significant movement by the federal government on the issue in years, but Hayes was neither satisfied nor finished.

"If it's a 'long-standing concern,'" Hayes asked in media interviews, "why hasn't something been done about it?" He also let it be known that he did not understand why Chao took more than three months to reply.

Hayes was a member of the National Advisory Committee on Occupational Safety and Health, an advisory body to OSHA, and he relentlessly used the power of his position to advocate for the health and safety of American workers. At NACOSH meetings, he spoke knowledgeably about the agency's years of inaction on data sheets reform, submitted written questions to Henshaw that he also made available to reporters, and in myriad ways pushed for action and accountability.

At the urging of Hayes, in March 2004 Sen. Michael Enzi (R-Wyo.), chairman of the Senate Health, Education, Labor and Pensions Committee's Subcommittee on Employment, Safety and Training, held a hearing on data sheets policy. Before becoming a senator, Enzi had been an accountant for an oil well company and there acquired first-hand knowledge about the shortcomings of data sheets.

Several witnesses testified that problems would be reduced if the United States adopted the Globally Harmonized System for Classification and Labeling of Chemicals (GHS), which is a proposed international standard for chemical hazard communication that requires pictographs and standardized warning language on data sheets. In November 2005, an Enzi spokesman said the senator would soon introduce legislation that would allow the U.S. to adopt GHS.

Ten days before Enzi's hearing, OSHA's Henshaw announced that he had completed the review requested by Chao and offered an initiative to improve data sheet accuracy. OSHA would issue some guidance materials to assist chemical manufacturers to prepare better sheets, and strengthen its enforcement efforts by giving its inspection officers lists of critical information that should appear on the data sheets of a handful of hazardous chemicals.

The enforcement aspect was indeed modest. Material safety data sheets are required for about 650,000 hazardous chemicals used in workplaces. OSHA said it would arm its inspectors with critical information for about 10 substances, less than one-hundredth of one percent of the hazardous chemicals the workforce encounters.

Small as these steps are, OSHA has not completed them. As this is being written in January 2006, two of the guidance documents are in the draft stage, one has not been issued even as a draft, and the inspectors are still waiting for the information on the 10 chemicals.

Meanwhile, though, the death toll mounts. As of late 2005, the Chemical Safety Board had issued reports on six separate accidents in which inaccurate data sheets were a factor, six tragedies that have taken the lives of 19 workers and injured 96 others.

I've filed 20 stories on data sheets through 2005 and have the satisfaction of knowing that I helped to raise the profile of an issue that has life or death consequences. In the last year, the American Industrial Hygiene Association, American Society of Safety Engineers, U.S. Chamber of Commerce, and National Association of Manufacturers have all weighed in publicly for data sheet reform. Whether OSHA gets the message remains to be seen.

—John Gannon

Job Safety

Ignorance of Safety Data Sheet Gaps Can Have Fatal Outcomes, Experts Say

By John Gannon

Evidence from a variety of expert sources suggests that a large proportion of material safety data sheets—which are supposed to provide essential health and safety information about hazardous chemicals in order that workers can handle them safely—are dangerously inaccurate.

According to the Occupational Safety and Health Administration, the information in the MSDSs can be trusted, but studies by the U.S. Chemical Safety and Hazardous Investigation Board and the Environmental Protection Agency, and even a study funded by OSHA itself, undermine that assumption, experts told BNA.

Since the Chemical Safety Board began operations in 1998, it has investigated 11 industrial chemical accidents. In three of these cases, the board has recommended that the information in the data sheets for the chemicals involved in the accidents be corrected in order to decrease the likelihood of similar tragedies in the future.

Morton International Explosion

Employees at the Morton International plant in Paterson, N.J., were trying to make a batch of dye on the night of April 8, 1998, when the kettle they were using exploded. The blast and fire injured nine workers, blew a hole through part of the facility's roof, and rained chemicals on surrounding neighborhoods.

In a report issued in August 2000, CSB concluded that the MSDS for the dye, Automate Yellow 96, was wrong on two counts. It listed the dye's National Fire Protection Association Reactivity Rating as zero (on a zero-to-four scale, with four being the most reactive), when it was actually one. Secondly, it listed the boiling point for Yellow 96 as 100 degrees when it in fact was about 330 degrees C.

In part because of the lack of accurate information about Yellow 96, the mixture in the kettle began to generate heat of its own and soon became uncontrollable. The operators stood by naively trying to cool the mixture at a time when they still had time to evacuate.

Bethlehem Steel Conflagration

At a Bethlehem Steel facility in Chesterton, Ind., on Feb. 2, 2001, while attempting to remove a cracked valve, workers opened a pipe containing coke oven gas condensate. According to CSB, Bethlehem Steel's MSDS for coke gas condensate indicated that it consists mostly of water. But coke oven gas condensate also contains a number of flammable components, such as benzene. The MSDS failed to state that if subjected to cold temperatures the nonflammable parts of the condensate can freeze while the flammable substances remain liquid.

The pipe that the crew opened had been partially frozen, and the liquid that flowed out was highly flammable. Two workers died, and four more were injured by the resulting fire.

CSB investigators determined the liquid may have been ignited by a nearby heat lamp or space heater. Had the crew known they might be dealing with a highly flammable liquid, they could have taken proper precautions before opening the pipe, board investigators suggested.

BP Amoco Molten Plastic Blast

On March 13, 2001, a maintenance technician and two assistants at the BP Amoco plant in Augusta, Ga. were killed while attempting to open the 1,750-pound cover of a catch tank for cleaning. Twelve hours before, the tank had been used in an unsuccessful attempt to make Amodel, a plastic used in automobiles and electronics. According to the board, available scientific literature on the material notes that it can generate large quantities of gas.

The cover was fastened to the tank around its circumference with 44 bolts. As the technician removed the twenty-second bolt, the pressure from the gas inside the tank ripped off the cover and hot plastic shot from the tank.

In its recommendations, the board suggested that the company, now Solvay Advanced Polymers, revise the MSDS for Amodel to warn past and future customers of its hazardous properties.

Struggle for Clarity

The Occupational Safety and Health Administration's hazard communication standard—29 CFR 1910.1200—requires chemical manufacturers and importers to provide MSDSs and employers to maintain them as part of a continuing program to protect workers.

In addition, Section 311 of the Emergency Planning and Community Right-To-Know Act requires employers to maintain material safety data sheets for hazardous chemicals kept at their facilities.

The information contained in an MSDS is supposed to help workers handle chemicals appropriately. In the event of a facility emergency or disaster, MSDSs are supposed to assist firefighters, hazardous materials teams, and health care professionals to address and resolve the crisis. MSDSs also allow citizens to learn about the properties of the chemicals that are used and stored in their communities.

A well-prepared MSDS offers clear answers to the following questions:

■ Do people using the chemical need special protective equipment?
■ Does the chemical emit fumes?
■ Does it ignite easily?
■ How can the chemical be stored safely?
■ How should it be handled in a facility fire?
■ Is it explosive?
■ Is it known or suspected to cause cancer?

OSHA Downplays Problem

In response to written questions from BNA, a spokeswoman for OSHA said the agency "rarely" finds inaccurate MSDSs during facility inspections and is not considering any actions to increase MSDS reliability, such as issuing a hazard information bulletin, increasing inspections, or proposing new regulations.

In Appendix E to OSHA's hazard communication standard, the agency says that employers can "rely on the information received from ... suppliers. You have no independent duty to analyze the chemical or evaluate the hazards of it."

Yet a study of 150 MSDSs funded by OSHA and published in the American Industrial Hygiene Journal in February 1995 found plenty of room to improve: only 37 percent had accurate health effects data, 47 percent had accurate information about personal protective equipment and occupational exposure limits, and 76 percent had adequate first aid information.

OSHA has not granted BNA's requests to interview OSHA officials further on the MSDS issue, although efforts to schedule an interview are ongoing.

Fred Blosser, a spokesman for the National Institute for Occupational Safety and Health, said the institute has never studied MSDS accuracy or been asked to study the issue by any government agency, labor, or trade organization. "It is not something that has crossed our radar screen," Blosser said.

Morton was originally fined $7,000 by OSHA for failing to provide a place of employment free from hazards, and settled with the agency for $5,000.

Bethlehem Steel was assessed $9,875 by the Indiana Department of Labor in proposed penalties for having a catwalk without a standard railing on all sides, not keeping the catwalk stairs clear of obstructions, not using lockout/tagout devices, and having power supply switches that were not arranged to be locked in the off position. Bethlehem Steel is contesting the fines.

Department spokeswoman Diane Mack said that the steelmaker was not cited for an inaccurate MSDS because the accident occurred on a Friday night and investigators did not arrive until the following Monday morning. By then, the liquid in question had evaporated, she said.

"Our agency needs a certain level of documentation to support a citation," Mack said.

The chemical board, because it has no enforcement power, was able to obtain a sample of coke oven gas condensate from an area of the facility close to where the accident occurred, and infer that the actual condensate involved in the fire was essentially similar, Mack said.

OSHA cited BP Amoco for exposing employees to the release of hazardous energy, failing to properly install pressure relief devices, and not training employees properly on lockout/tagout procedures. It originally proposed fines of $141,000 and settled the case for $119,000.

A senior OSHA official familiar with the agency's investigation said that investigators did not seek to determine if the MSDS for Amodel was correct.

"Not being chemists, I don't think we looked into it that deeply," he said.

EPA Issues Alert

The issue of MSDS accuracy has crossed the radar of the Environmental Protection Agency. In a chemical safety alert issued in June 1999, "Use Multiple Data Sources for Safer Emergency Response," EPA cautioned emergency responders that the information in a single MSDS should not be trusted when planning a response to a facility emergency, such as a fire. The alert cited incidents in Arkansas and Lodi, N.J., in which firefighters and emergency responders depended on an MSDS to make a critical decision, and lost their lives as a result.

To illustrate the point, EPA obtained MSDSs for the insecticide azinphos methyl (CAS No. 86-50-0) from four different suppliers. The four documents offered conflicting views of the substance's flammability, incompatibilities, reactivity, and overall hazard ratings. One MSDS listed "high temperatures, oxidizers, alkaline substances" as incompatible with the insecticide; a second said "acids and bases" were incompatible; and a third cited "heat, moisture."

The alert also noted that "vagueness, technical jargon, understandability, product vs. process concerns, and missing information on an MSDS may increase the risk to emergency responders."

In an October 2001 safety alert, the American Institute of Chemical Engineers' Center for Chemical Process Safety warned that "MSDS for the same material but from different sources can vary considerably in what they report as hazards."

Chorus of Criticism

Union representatives and others involved with workplace safety say that while some MSDS are wrong or lack critical information, others are full of confusing, contradictory, and obscure language.

"There is something seriously wrong here," said Diane Stein, a safety specialist with the Paper, Allied-Industrial, Chemical & Energy Workers International Union (PACE). "We don't want to trash MSDSs entirely. There is a lot of useful information in them. We would like to see some improvements."

"MSDSs are really weak," said Mark Dudzic, president of the PACE local for the Morton facility. "You can't rely on them."

Mark Roehler, a chemical technologist and principal in Lehder, a Canadian environmental and safety consulting firm, said that many MSDSs are written to fulfill the letter of the law rather than the spirit of providing useful information. Lehder helps organizations such as schools determine if their MSDSs are accurate, and lobbies the supplier to correct the information if it is wrong.

"It doesn't surprise me that people can get hurt with faulty information, but I couldn't give you a percentage of how often they are inaccurate," Roehler said. "I've seen a lot of really bad MSDSs over the years."

Michael Wright, director of health, safety, and environment for the United Steelworkers, said it is not uncommon to find this stock phrase on an MSDS: "Nothing in this mixture is hazardous under 29 CFR 1910.1200."

Wright noted that the same MSDS also may advise that the chemical be used with adequate ventilation, skin contact be avoided, vapors not be inhaled, and respiratory protection approved by the

National Institute for Occupational Safety and Health be used.

"What's the message here?" Wright asked. "It's not hazardous, but don't let it get near you."

Wright said USW was asked by one of its locals to evaluate MSDSs for ceramic fibers produced by two manufacturers. Although the products were similar, the first manufacturer's MSDS included the phrase "Warning: Causes Cancer." The second MSDS said, "Note: This material has been associated with malignant and nonmalignant neoplasms in experimental animals via interperitoneal installation. As this route of exposure does not mimic the human experience, the significance of this finding is uncertain."

Although manufacturers are required to include warnings on MSDSs if the material is a possible human carcinogen, the law does not prohibit using technical language that few people will understand.

Old Problem, Unions Say

Although OSHA contends that faulty MSDSs are rare, and NIOSH has not studied the issue, PACE's Stein contends the problem is not new.

"People involved in the labor movement have been working on this for a long time," she said.

When teaching worker safety classes, Stein uses materials prepared by the Labor Institute that cite a 1986 study by David Chawes, an industrial hygienist who reviewed more than 450 MSDSs for hazardous substances used by health care workers. Chawes found that more than half of the documents left blanks in places where there was supposed to be information, and 30 percent lacked internal consistency, such as stating that the substance was not hazardous while advising the use of a respirator. Less than 3 percent of all the MSDSs were judged to be of a quality acceptable for employees to use.

"Employees are taught to rely on the MSDS as the source of hazard information, yet few MSDSs stand up to even simple scrutiny," Chawes wrote.

A spokesman for the New York-based Labor Institute said the materials are used in union worker safety programs that are funded by grants from OSHA, the National Institute for Environmental

Health Science, and various state agencies. He estimated that at least 25,000 workers have been trained with the materials.

Warning Signs

Although Chawes, Roehler, and Wright note that many of the mistakes found on MSDSs only can be detected by a person with some knowledge of chemistry, they note that sometimes there are obvious signals that something is wrong:

Brevity: Two different manufacturers make the same substance. One provides a 12-page MSDS and the other just three pages. The brevity of the second MSDS should be an alert that the manufacturer may not be providing all relevant information, according to Roehler.

Inconsistency: An example from Chawes is a product described as a liquid in one place, but discussed in another part of the document as if it is a gas.

Technical Jargon: On May 4, 1988, a plant owned by the Pacific Engineering & Production Co. in Henderson, Nev., was leveled by a series of explosions. The blasts killed two employees, injured 350 workers and local residents, and caused property damage up to 12 miles away, according to a report prepared by the USW. The facility made ammonium perchlorate, an oxidant used in rockets and missiles.

The blasts were caused by a fire that ignited the ammonium perchlorate. Nowhere on the two-page MSDS prepared by the company was the material described as explosive. The document states simply that "spontaneous decomposition will occur" if the material is heated above 300 degrees C. According to the report, federal investigators later rated the total force of the explosions generated by the decomposition as equivalent to 340 tons of TNT.

Use Multiple Information Sources

In its safety alert, EPA suggested obtaining information about each hazardous material from several sources. A number of chemical information sources are available on the Internet, including:

Computer-Aided Management of Emergency Operations (CAMEO): This software is available from EPA at http://www.epa.gov/ceppo/cameo/what.htm. CAMEO uses a chemical database of over 6,000 substances with chemical-specific information on hazards and controls.

ChemFinder.Com: A World Wide Web server at http://chemfinder.cambridgesoft.com/ contains information on about 75,000 compounds. The information is maintained by the CambridgeSoft Corp., a supplier of life science software and chemical databases.

Vermont Safety Information Resources Inc.: The Web site at http://www.hazard.com/msds/index.php operated by this small nonprofit contains MSDSs and links to MSDSs for about 200,000 chemicals.

International Programme on Chemical Safety: This NIOSH Web site at http://www.cdc.gov/niosh/ipcs/ipcscard.html contains international chemical safety cards for about 1,400 chemicals commonly found in the workplace. The cards provide much of the same information as an MSDS in an easier-to-understand format.

OSHA Rule Lists Requirements

OSHA's requirements for MSDS can be found at 29 CFR 1910.1200 (g). The requirements include the following: the chemical and common names of all ingredients which have been determined to be health hazards; physical and chemical characteristics (such as vapor pressure, flashpoint); physical hazards (potential for fire, explosion, and reactivity); health hazards; primary routes of entry into human beings; permissable exposure limits; whether the chemical is listed as a carcinogen; precautions for safe handling and use (including protective measures during repair and maintenance of contaminated equipment); applicable control measures (such as appropriate engineering controls, personal protective equipment); emergency and first aid procedures; date of preparation of the MSDS, contact information for the party responsible for preparing the MSDS.

There is also a voluntary standard for preparing MSDSs published by the American National Standards Institute (ANZI Z400.1-1998), which is available for purchase for $100 from http://ansi.org/.

Reproduced with permission from Daily Report for Executives, *No. 113, pp. C-1 - C-4 (June 12, 2002). Copyright 2002 by The Bureau of National Affairs, Inc., 800/372-1033, www.bna.com.*

JOURNALISM
THAT
MATTERS

Chapter 5

Judging the Judges

The Lord Chief Justice of England and Wales, reacting to a Legal
Business *piece, tells the Technology & Construction Court to shape up*

Judges on the United Kingdom's Technology and Construction Court
hear some of the world's most complicated and high-value commercial disputes, but some lawyers had begun to feel that the judges were
failing the public. Establishing and publishing the depth of disenchant-
ment with the court was a colossal task, but once we did so, change followed. We can say with some satisfaction that the restructuring of the
court which arose as a result of publication has made the court a very
different place from what it was before. The Lord Chief Justice of
England and Wales took steps to confirm our findings, then instituted
an unprecedented court shake-up.

The idea of running a story on judges evolved gradually. At the
prompting of a number of senior lawyers, I'd started taking an interest
in the workings of the judiciary soon after becoming litigation correspondent on *Legal Business* magazine. For someone who can't see a wall
without wanting to grab a ladder and look over the top, it provided a
lengthy period of fascination.

To understand the significance of the story, and why it appealed to
me, a bit of background on the peculiarities of English judges might be
helpful. Our judges—perhaps rightly—view themselves as the most
independent in the world. It is certainly the case that they are answerable to no one. Judges are not appraised, nor do they have their work
reviewed. It's a solitary existence where by and large they are forbid-

den from discussing their work and receive little administrative support in writing judgments.

But it's not all drudgery and loneliness. The judiciary is the third branch of government and makes a lot of law. As such it is a position of power and privilege. On a daily basis a judge might fine, imprison, or deport a man. They might take away his kids or his house. To execute such tasks with fairness and equanimity is a formidable responsibility, demanding near-superhuman qualities of those society entrusts with this task. Thus the public expects its judges to be different from those they judge. Judges, too, believe in their own superiority and virtue: "Once a man becomes a judge he has nothing to gain from further promotion," Lord Denning, former Master of the Rolls, once said, "and does not seek it."

I thought this traditionalist view of judges somewhat fanciful and began to suspect that somewhere on the Bench I'd find someone less than virgin-pure, perhaps even a racist, a lecher, or a liar. In a notoriously cynical age, would the public willingly invest so much trust in the judiciary if they knew what their judges were really like? I thought I'd try to find out.

I limited my inquiry to judges' conduct in court and hoped to expose those failing the public. It was no easy task: judges don't talk to the press, appear on television, or invite discussion on aspects of their jobs like sentencing. I was fortunate in that my job gave me access to many of the country's most influential lawyers. If anyone could help draw an accurate picture of the judiciary at work, they could. I was not, however, naïve enough to expect them to rush forward with attributable criticism. It would be a breach of the unwritten code which forbids lawyers criticizing judges and judges from criticizing each other. Secondly, many senior barristers ultimately aspire to being made judges themselves; I was asking them to burn down the very club they wanted to join. Last and most important, those whose opinions I attached most value to — those with near daily contact with the judges concerned — would for obvious reasons be unemployable as advocates if it became public that they thought the judge hearing their next trial was an alcoholic, say.

The obvious solution was to run their remarks anonymously, but that is not a preferred approach. *Legal Business* has always maintained clear ethical standards. Our policy is never to present the most damning or most critical evidence in a story without attribution. Although I felt I would find a great story, doing so while meeting our standards would present a formidable hurdle. The answer was to survey lawyers and report the results in the aggregate. Although we would be granting them anonymity, we at least had control over who received the questionnaires. The risk in granting anonymity is that it reduces accountability: at worst we could have been fed deliberately misleading information. We could counter this in two ways. First, among the small and knowledgeable elite I had a contact who in true Deep Throat fashion would confirm or question the accuracy of information I collected. Secondly, a common-sense approach led us to filter out suspiciously good reviews or markedly bad. In most cases a clear and consistent picture of the merits and demerits of each appeared. Where this was a negative picture, I put the criticism before the judges, giving them a chance to respond. Some did respond; others never returned calls, but none would comment on the record.

With our method settled, we mailed members of niche barristers' chambers — lawyers who work in offices specializing in certain areas of law — whom we knew were familiar with the judges and asked them to complete questionnaires. In them we sought views on judges' legal and technical abilities; the fairness, courtesy, and sensitivity they showed while sitting and also their ability to manage the case and courtroom.

Legal Business published the findings of these surveys in three issues spread over a 12-month period. The first, and arguably the most provocative, concerned the judiciary of the Chancery Division. We faithfully reported the view of the users of the court that one judge, a recent appointee, was widely perceived to be "pompous," "gratuitously rude," "conceited," "bullying," and absolutely blind to his own

Legal Business

www.legalbusiness.co.uk

Established: 1990

Publisher: Legalease, London

Frequency: Monthly

Characteristics: Four color magazine

Circulation: 9,000, paid subscription

Readership: Legal professionals in the U.K., Europe, Asia, and U.S.

Editorial staff: 12

faults. The judge concerned had declined to respond when offered the opportunity, but I was subsequently made aware that he was furious about the article. To make matters worse, a number of the national newspapers ran short stories about its findings. We hung on wondering if he might resign (judges are sacked at the rate of one every other century). In the meantime I received a number of anonymous calls asking about the veracity of my sources and whether I was aware of the seriousness of what I'd done. In the end, though, nothing spectacular came of it.

We felt that the mere publication of the survey served some purpose: it sent a message to the judges on the Bench that while they were not accountable to an employer as such, the worst excesses of their behavior could and would be exposed. It was a novelty to most judges to have any feedback on their performance.

Once the dust had settled we ran another survey, this time covering the Queen's Bench Division of the High Court. Although the judges were almost exclusively white, public school and Oxbridge-educated, it appeared that the standard of judging in this division was meeting expectations. I concede that this was something of a disappointment; I'd hoped to uncover something a little more controversial.

We next covered the Technology and Construction Court (TCC). The TCC had been in my sights for some time: I'd been told by a mediator that he could always settle a construction dispute because the alternative was going before the TCC, where seven out of the nine sitting judges were incompetent. It was a throwaway comment, but one worth following up.

The survey into the TCC turned up a number of problems with the court, the bulk of which were not immediately related to the competence of the judges themselves. The issues were magnified because of the court's commercial significance and status. The construction industry in the UK makes up 10 percent of GDP. Secondly, the UK has long been established as a hub of international dispute resolution, and the TCC is the only specialist court of its type in the world. It became evident that in a litigious industry like construction, the proper functioning of this court was vital to a multi-billion dollar construction industry worldwide. Oh, and the court also handled colossal technology claims.

The result of the survey turned up the stark fact that frequent users of the court would do anything in their power to have their cases heard before other divisions of the High Court rather than take them before the specialist TCC. We were able to supplement the anonymous opinions of frequent court users with on-the-record quotes from trade bodies associated with the court and construction industry. The picture it painted was grim: although when set up, it was regarded as trailblazing and innovative court, twenty years on, it had lost its way. The single biggest influence on this decline was the status of the judges. Although the TCC heard some of the highest-value cases in the UK, and was responsible for making a lot of new law, those on the bench were Senior Circuit judges rather than full High Court judges. If the best and the brightest judges are recruited to the ranks of the High Court, it necessarily follows that Senior Circuit judges are not. The Department for Constitutional Affairs (DCA) had no reason for this: like much in our system of justice, it was simply an historic anomaly that begged to be corrected.

Additionally we found that the court's image was seriously handicapped by the continued presence of one judge in particular, His Honor Judge Seymour, who was perceived as being not up to the job.

We published our findings in November 2004, but the full impact of the story did not become apparent until early June 2005. A press release from the DCA announced in early June that High Court judges — for the first time in history — were to be appointed to the TCC. I immediately wondered if the article had influenced the DCA's decision, not least because the press release appeared to paraphrase a succession of points made in the article.

The day after the announcement I was given an account (not for attribution, naturally) of how these changes had come about. Someone had drawn the attention of the Lord Chief Justice of England and Wales to the article and our finding that the court was failing. He subsequently sent his deputy to investigate whether or not the claims made in the article stood up. The various users' committees were assembled, given copies of the article, and asked whether what we'd published reflected their experience. Happily for me they endorsed the article's findings. The DCA decided to act, and did so swiftly.

In addition to rectifying the anomaly over the status of the judges, the DCA had also kicked His Honor Judge Seymour out of the TCC. In all honesty you need to know the legal profession to appreciate the magnitude of these changes. The pace of change in the law, infrequently and reluctantly undertaken, is usually incredibly slow. Change also implies that things before were less than perfect, and lawyers are often too arrogant to contemplate such a scenario.

Having heard the inside story about how the *Legal Business* piece was used by the government to bring about positive change, I was naturally keen for it to be recognized. I called some of the sources who had helped with the original story and for once got a QC (Queen's Counsel) to go on the record: "I am clear that last year's *Legal Business* article was the catalyst for a review of the court and its composition." Job done.

—*Matthew Rushton*

Technology and Construction Court Judges

Courting Criticism

The Court of Appeal publicly slated a Technology and Construction Court judge earlier this year. Seemingly far from its trailblazing roots, has it lost its way?

By Matthew Rushton

Since the court of appeal turned its guns on His Honour Judge Richard Seymour in January 2004, the judiciary of the Technology and Construction Court (TCC) have been scrutinised intently. Barristers and solicitors who spoke "off the record" to Legal Business offered critiques of the Bench that, in the worse cases, ranged from "petulant" and "over-political", to "gratuitously rude".

Now, everyone has an opinion, which often gets more colourful behind a veil of anonymity, but the situation at the TCC seems serious. In the course of researching this article, LB contacted a representative cross section of the court's stakeholders. Among them are the chairmen of the Technology and Construction Solicitors Association (TeCSA) and Tecbar, whose views by far represent the largest vested interest in the Court's good functioning. Senior construction QCs from recognised sets were also consulted, as were regional and London-based solicitors.

Good Foundations

The TCC is crucial to UK business, and its users are unhappy with some of its judges. Look at the facts: it is the only specialist construction court in the world, and serves an industry that makes up 10% of UK gross domestic product. In a sector where bustups are as common as house bricks, an effective means of resolving disputes is no less vital than cement.

The degree of sector-specialisation offered by the English courts, however, brings its own burdens. Three factors make life on the TCC bench a more gruelling prospect than might be expected in other divisions:

■ First is the emotive nature of construction disputes. All disputes are emotional, but construction brings a unique set of dynamics into play. "In construction, it's possible to act in reasonably good faith and still find yourself in a big hole," says one partner at a leading firm. "When you are in that hole you still have the risk, you still have to perform and you are still responsible to people further up the chain." The pressure is unrelenting. Despite the vast sums committed to major projects, construction companies operate on slender margins and are not cash-rich; money to throw at litigation, understandably, is resented all the more.

■ Secondly, construction law is a minefield. The legal complexities of construction litigation are seldom appreciated by those outside the industry. "Over the years the TCC has been dealing with some of largest, most complicated and legally groundbreaking cases," says Peter Rees, Norton Rose's head of litigation, and chairman of TeCSA. "A lot of the cases that have changed the approach to the law on tort, and negligence in particular, have come from the TCC," he says. "Law progresses in many cases thanks to construction," adds Lovells partner Melanie Willems. "Many key decisions in recent years have had a construction element to them. It's a situation where you get a number of parties involved, all with different concerns, all fighting for justice. Trying to balance out people's rights and remedies is a huge headache – you're taking law to the limit in interpreting what many contracts, as drafted, and indeed some legislation, mean in this context."

■ The third burden on the TCC judiciary is the fact that they act as the court of appeal from arbitrators' decisions and as the court that enforces adjudicators' decisions. In the latter area alone the TCC has produced around 120 reported decisions in the past five years.

Maintaining the confidence of the industry and users of the

Court in each of these areas requires extra-judicial aptitudes. It is a curious anomaly, therefore, that those on whom these burdens fall should not be High Court judges, but (hierarchically inferior) senior circuit judges. Anomalies aside, the Court has excelled in the past. Its contribution to case law over the years is undoubted. Likewise, when Lord Woolf was looking at ways to improve case management for the new Civil Procedure Rules, he turned to the TCC. Woolf adopted many of the hands-on case management techniques developed by the Court in the 1980s, which are now regarded as a central feature of the rules.

But so much for history. A glorious past is no guarantee of a glorious future, as trial judge Richard Seymour's actions last year displayed so visibly. The judiciary, practitioners and clients have for some time been conscious of a need to restore public confidence in the ability and competence of the Court.

See Less Seymour

A turning point in the Court's history came in January with the Court of Appeal's decision in Cooperative Group (CWS) Ltd v International Computers Ltd. CWS v ICL, as it became known, gave critics of the TCC all the ammunition they needed. Where previously their criticisms could be dismissed as the griping of disappointed litigants, now their complaints were in the public domain and judicially endorsed. In ordering a retrial, the Court of Appeal's findings concerned the conduct of trial judge, His Honour Judge Richard Seymour. They were a blow to the Court: so strongly worded as to risk long-term harm of the Court's reputation.

Tuckey LJ, Rix LJ and Parker LJ stated the following damning words:

'The trial judge had erred so fundamentally in his approach to the trial as to have lost, or at least given the appearance of losing, his ability to try CWS's claim with an objective judicial mind. It was not that he had come to the trial with any preconceived prejudice or predilection or bias, but that, over the course of it, he had demonstrated an inability to grapple objectively with the issues of fact and law presented to him. In the result the trial had been unfair. The judge had made findings of bad faith and false evidence, against CWS, its principal witness, and a CWS employee who was not even a witness, when no bad faith had been suggested or pleaded, and then had inevitably been drawn into utilising his conclusions about CWS or its employees' bad faith for the purpose of deciding other disputed issues of fact and law. The focus of the trial judge's objective vision was distorted.'

The effects of Judge Seymour's conduct on the court are perhaps matched only by the suffering of Richard Mawrey QC, a senior and well-respected silk from Henderson Chambers, who represented CWS. In concluding his first-instance judgment, Judge Seymour saw fit to name and rubbish counsel in the most high-handed and insulting terms. This streak of gratuitous rudeness is said by others to feature in several of his judgments, and be consistent with his manner, at times, in Court.

On the penultimate page of his 193-page judgment, Judge Seymour wrote: 'The formidable problems of showing a contract seem never to have been seriously addressed before the trial of this action, and even at trial, Mr Mawrey showed no enthusiasm for grappling with them. The whole focus of CWS's case was how outrageous it was that ICL could have conducted itself as it did, as if indignation would carry the claims forward past the legal and factual difficulties... The approach to considering the quality of the evidence as to causation of alleged loss of profits was in my judgment so far deficient as to involve a wholesale suspension of disbelief when looking at what conclusions could be fairly drawn from the results of the Harlech trial.'

Of the numerous sources consulted for this article, Judge Seymour emerged as the division's most criticised judge. One law firm partner found some Woolfian positives out of it, describing the drastic reaction to finding out Seymour was slated for his client's trial. 'There was no way we wanted that man anywhere near our clients' problems and both sides settled immediately,' he recalls. 'We just had to look at each other and say however painful this is going to be, it's going to involve a lot less pain than he would inflict on both of us.'

However, when he does take his seat on the bench, Seymour's talents are also hard to miss: he is undoubtedly (and prodigiously) clever, and similarly hard working. His judgments are delivered promptly and in impressive volume. Over the 2003 calendar year, Judge Seymour produced 18 judgments; Judge Thornton was the only other judge in the division to hand down more than six. Even so, his record of being over-turned on appeal alone should be cause for concern. Over that year, the Court of Appeal heard seven appeals from cases handled by Seymour and allowed four of them. Were these statistics to include the CWS v ICL appeal, on recent form Seymour would have had almost half his decisions appealed, and half of those allowed.

Reasons To Worry

The Seymour saga is problematic for this key Court. It's reflected in a groundswell of advocates' opinion that says if you can get your case before any of the other divisions, then do so. 'More and more people are avoiding the Court – not because it isn't in principle a good system, but because there are one or two people who are just loopy,' one solicitor says.

Another adds: 'As a practising lawyer I can tell you, you go into court with your heart in your mouth; you have your fingers crossed thinking I hope I don't get so and so.' Users of the Court have several grumbles that are so grouped:

■ Consistency

Most prominent of the issues likely to repel potential litigants is consistency. Wide disparities in approach between judges have been apparent for some time. 'The problem with inconsistency,' Peter Rees says, 'is that clients expect you, as an experienced litigator, to know how the Court is going to approach a particular problem. If you're not able to predict that for the client, there's a problem. The client begins to wonder whether you are as competent as you should be, or whether the Court is not as competent as it should be.'

Inconsistency appears in three main areas. According to reputable sources, the Court has regularly erred in achieving consistency in case and trial management; in decision making, (particularly as concerns adjudication); and in the personal idiosyncrasies of the judges.

■ Case management

On case management, one solicitor voices a typical complaint. 'There has never been any consistency – it's very much down to the individual whim of the particular judge. You often get the case where the parties arrive at a case management conference having agreed directions, and the judge will disregard the wishes of the parties entirely, sometimes setting completely unrealistic timetables instead. It varies enormously from judge to judge, so you can never really advise your client what is likely to happen.'

Responding to such complaints, one judge from the division says: 'We are aware of the need to be concerned to avoid inconsistency in case management, but I'm not conscious at the moment of any specific concern that needs particularly to be addressed. I'd be alive to any suggestions that there may be.' Alleged inconsistency in case management has been a long-running theme in the TCC. Two years ago the presiding judge Mr Justice Forbes met members of TeCSA and Tecbar to request that any concerns, if not formal complaints, be brought before the Court. Identification of specific inconsistencies, however, was not forthcoming.

The judges for their part meet regularly to discuss questions of case management and a users' committee comprising four solicitors and eight non-lawyers also sits as a forum to discuss issues such as this. The palpable and near-uniform dissatisfaction among users that was expressed to *Legal Business* over case management sits uneasily with the Court's own perception of the problem. Despite the appearance of strong communication between the users and the Bench, it seems inevitable that rumours will persist until a means is found for users to articulate negative feedback without adversely affecting their careers.

One argument frequently cited in defence of the judges is that those lawyers who make the complaints are simply unused to hands-on case management.

But as other divisions of the Court now take a similar approach, the pool users to whom this applies will diminish substantially over time.

■ Adjudication

Inconsistency concerning adjudication is the main focus of criticism on decisions. Outside this area, users are more complimentary. 'On the whole, the Court produces very few barking decisions,' says one QC.

The new battleground in adjudication has been enforcement proceedings. One judge describes it as 'a micro-climate of law', and, as mentioned above, the TCC has produced around 120 reported decisions in adjudication over the past five years.

But some users sense that judicial approval of adjudication is by no means universal. The colossal success of adjudication has without doubt robbed the Court of substantial amounts of work. In tandem with Woolf's pre-action protocols, work levels in the TCC have fallen significantly in recent years. While this has enabled litigants to get to court quickly, and the judges to issue judgments promptly, a certain tension between the traditional and new means of dispute resolution has been noted. 'The recent decisions by the TCC on adjudication have basically been absurd,' says one solicitor. 'I had a case recently where the judge sat there griping on about adjudication, what a ludicrous thing it was, how it was intended only for small cases and big cases weren't supposed to be referred. All of this was off the top of his head because, whether he likes it or not, it's not what the Act says.'

(Nothing in the Arbitration Act 1996 states that only certain types of dispute can be referred. The impression the judge's behaviour left on the parties was that of sour grapes – he'd rather be dealing with this interesting and complex case himself.) Responding on behalf of the judiciary, one judge concedes: 'There are, I'm sure, examples where individual judges on specific points appear to be in disagreement with each other, but I'd have thought overall the general view of the way the Act and process has been interpreted by the Court has been reasonably well received by the users.'

'Overall the Court has been supportive of adjudication and helped it bed down in what is now a clearly established method of dispute resolution,' he adds.

■ Idiosyncrasies

The personal idiosyncrasies of the TCC judiciary are well known to the Court's users, and arguably play a greater role because the pool of available judges is comparatively smaller than in other divisions. Making light of what many see as a serious issue, one QC points out its advantages: 'They're all different and it needs standardisation, but, if you've got a particularly demanding legal question that requires rigorous analysis, then Humphrey Lloyd's your man; if however you want a straightforward view on the merits of a case, you'd want Wilcox in charge.'

Commenting on the judges' varied approaches, while also making a wider point about the competence of the Court, one solicitor says: 'There are cases I can think of, and some that I'm involved in, where claimants have tried to take their cases before other divisions – the perception is that the TCC's a bit of a lottery. You wouldn't want your cases before certain judges unless you had a really bad case, in which case they might take a decision in your favour.'

Whatever the predilections and idiosyncrasies of the TCC judiciary, their significance to one of the UK's biggest industries and the legal community at large, by common consent, merits greater recognition in status terms. It is a puzzling anomaly that, since 1998, the presiding head of the TCC has been a full High Court judge, but the remainder are not.

Shortly after New Labour swept to power in 1997, what was then known as the Official Referees Court was renamed the Technology and Construction Court. In a breezy press release, then Lord Chancellor Lord Irvine announced: 'From today, the Official Referees will be known as the Judges of the Technology and Construction Court. They will be addressed as "My Lord" instead of "Your Honour". This reflects the fact that, although not High Court Judges, they invariably sit in the High Court and try complex High Court cases.'

Being addressed as 'Your Honour' might indeed be flattering, but it's slender compensation for a salary £30,000 per annum below that of a High Court judge, to say nothing of the pension provisions. The status of the judiciary affects the Court in a number of ways.

'It has traditionally distorted the selection process,' says Paul Darling QC, chairman of Tecbar. 'It gives rise to a perception of a two-tier system, with the TCC perceived to be in the second tier.' It is both an issue of quality and perception. 'In the long term,' he adds, 'the only solution is for the Court to be staffed by judges with High Court status. It's a disgrace that this has not yet happened.'

Rectifying what is commonly regarded as an historic anomaly can be approached in two ways: either immediately through converting the existing judges, or through ensuring that all new judges recruited to the TCC are High Court judges. Having pushed for the former to no avail, TeCSA is at least hoping for the latter. 'We would like to see new judges who are appointed to the TCC being High Court judges because it seems to me that this is one way of bringing about change,' Peter Rees says.

Perceptions aside, it is beyond question that those on the TCC Bench would perform better were they afforded the same level of administrative support that High Court judges enjoy. Currently each TCC judge is allocated a clerk, who, in civil service terms, is an executive officer. They are required to sit in court all day, act as a listings officer, and also be a point of contact between the users for the court and the court system. As such they have little time for clerking the judges.

The matter lies with the Department for Constitutional Affairs. And there it lies. A spokesman for the Department confirmed that no consideration is currently being given to changing the status quo.

Matters may yet come to a head, however, when the new Commercial Court building comes on stream in October 2008. The new building will bring the Commercial Court, the Admiralty Court and the TCC under the same roof. 'It would make practical sense,' Rees says, 'for there to be three separate lists: commercial, admiralty, and TCC, and for there to be, on occasions, a swap over, so if the Commercial Court is particularly overstretched then a judge from the admiralty list or a TCC judge could help out.'

While accepting users might find the situation 'a little strange,' one TCC judge says, 'you only have to look at the cause list any day in the QBD to see there are more circuit judges sitting as deputy High Court judges trying Queen's Bench actions than there are High Court judges.' As such, he says, 'it is only an aspect of a wider anomaly of the judicial system generally'.

Seymour's Fate

While the Seymour debacle will doubtless continue to stigmatise the court for some time, the TCC is far from a dead-loss. With few exceptions, the judiciary is highly intelligent, well intentioned and hard working. The various users committees and trade bodies are approachable, concerned and motivated. Those involved have been upfront about the Court's shortcomings and those implicated show a remarkable willingness to change and adapt as required.

In September 2004, Mr Justice Jackson succeeded Mr Justice Forbes as presiding judge of the division, following the end of Forbes J's term of office. While no criticism is made of Mr Justice Forbes, Mr Justice Jackson's appointment has been greeted with near-universal enthusiasm. The co-author and now consultant editor of the leading text, Jackson and Powell on Professional Negligence, Jackson is regarded as a formidable intellect with a sterling pedigree at the Bar and on the Bench. While his plans at present remain confidential, it is known that he has an agenda for change.

A skeptical constituency is keen to see results.

Reproduced with permission from Legal Business.

JOURNALISM
THAT
MATTERS

Chapter 6

Off the Critical Path

Software makers, challenged by Engineering News-Record, *close a hole that lets schedulers manipulate construction timing*

In 2003 four veteran project scheduling consultants approached Richard Korman, a senior business editor at *Engineering News-Record*, with a story that for their industry would be, if not a bombshell, at least something highly contentious. Construction project schedulers were using flexibility features built into leading project scheduling software to make timelines come out the way they wanted them to— not how they were supposed to come out under the established standards of what's known as the critical path method (CPM) of scheduling.

Outside the construction industry the issue would hardly arouse anyone's attention, but enormous safety, legal, and financial matters hinge on the integrity of the scheduling that goes into a project. The issue of what part of a project can be done when is all-important. You can't hang the glass exterior walls of a building before you erect the frame, and you can't erect the frame until you have the materials and the workers to do it. Delays and inefficiencies arise anytime there's a snag in the order of events, so ad-hoc tinkering with scheduling is a best-practices no-no.

Given the stakes, Korman knew he had the potential for a hot story when the experts—James O'Brien, Fredric Plotnick, Stuart Ockman, and Jon Wickwire approached him about concerns they had with the flexibility features in the software, including the leading software in the industry. By enabling schedulers to manipulate the schedule, Korman says the executives told him, the software "robbed the process of integrity."

At the root of the issue was a switch by software companies from a feature used in original CPM software called the arrow diagramming method (ADM) to one called the precedence diagramming method (PDM), the former creating more rigid schedules, the latter, more flexible ones. With their increased flexibility, schedulers could assign different calendars to different activities, so if certain activities were included on the same "logic path" as other activities, they wouldn't show up with the same amount of "float," the term for building in a time cushion. The time cushion is crucial in a schedule, because it helps engineers deal with delays before they hold up other aspects of the job.

Assigning different calendars to activities is "like saying the grass is not green anymore to a classically trained scheduler from the 1960s, '70s and maybe early '80s," says Ockman, one of the experts who alerted Korman. Although the experts don't blame the software makers, since changes to PDM were rooted in changes in other software products and were made over the years to meet client demand, the migration has caused problems. "The fact is that the primary de facto standard (that all the software companies are following) has prevented CPM from being practiced the way the inventors created it."

In one example from a few years ago, a contractor simply shortened the duration of activities in the later

Engineering News-Record

www.enr.com

Established: 1874

Publisher: The McGraw-Hill Companies, Inc., New York

Frequency: Weekly

Characteristics: Four-color, average 74 pages

Circulation: 71,000

Readership: Contractors, engineers, architects, owners, city, state and federal government officials, producers, suppliers, colleges, and libraries

Editorial staff: Editor-in-chief, two managing editors, two editors-at-large, six senior editors, three associate editors, two assistant editors, two news bureau chiefs, 24 correspondents, two researchers, production manager and two production assistants, art director, three associate art directors, three database coordinators

stages of a project when work fell behind on the early phases. Such a move goes against good scheduling practices, which call for early and monthly updates, including performing forward or backward passes through the entire project, if early delays threaten to slow down later stages of a project. To simply speed up scheduling of later-stage steps defies accepted industry practices.

For Korman, a crucial point in determining the seriousness of what the experts were saying was their credibility. All of them were something of elder statesmen in the industry and cofounders of the College of Scheduling, a program for project schedulers at the Project Management Institute, an international professional development society based in Newtown Square, Pa. O'Brien had helped invent modern CPM.

Even so, Korman at first questioned whether the experts were truly speaking for the industry or just throwbacks from an earlier era, purists who might be a bit "out of touch with reality," Korman says.

Korman's boss, Janice Tuchman, editor-in-chief of *ENR*, shared his hesitation. "My concern was that we be sure that Richard's sources were not a minority opinion, but really represented industry thinking," says Tuchman.

Korman decided to pursue the story to see what others were saying. Because this was unfamiliar territory—his regular beat was business, not technology—and the subject matter was complex, he conducted extensive background research.

After interviewing industry experts and educators well-versed in the minutiae of CPM scheduling software and the theory behind it—CPM is based on mathematical principals—he began to think O'Brien and his colleagues had a strong case. Korman and Tuchman had periodic conversations to determine the importance of the story, and Tuchman was still wary of "irresponsibly representing the views of a few people who were out of touch with the marketplace," Korman says. However, he kept coming back to the issue, saying "here's evidence. It's true."

When Korman called a representative from the leading software company to get its reactions to O'Brien's claims, the call wasn't an easy one. "They weren't happy," says Korman, in part because his call meant that the four experts, who had previously made their concerns known to the company, had decided to go public—through *ENR*.

After weighing his research and the comments from his sources, Korman decided the issue was valid. Tuchman gave him the go-ahead, and Korman worked with a freelancer, Stephen Daniels, to write the piece, "Critics Can't Find the Logic in Many of Today's CPM Schedules," for the May 26, 2003, issue of *ENR*. In it, Korman and Daniels talked about the controversial software features, but they also aired the issue from the point of view of schedulers and others who support the flexibility features.

Although they had been concerned about being pressured not to publish the piece, which was sure to be controversial and would involve big advertisers (the main software company was a regular, and prominent, advertiser), Tuchman never told Korman to "tip-toe" around advertisers. In this case, no pressure came, and the software company never threatened to pull its ads. The main company, says Tuchman, "just rolled with it," and explained their point of view for the story.

Korman's experience and *ENR*'s resources were a plus in tackling the piece. Korman had been with *ENR* for 20 years, giving him the experience and credibility to tackle the story, and *ENR* has access to a team of lawyers because the publication is so accustomed to controversy. "I've been sued once and subpoenaed twice," Korman notes. "The publication has a supportive environment."

Tuchman says it's the job of B-2-B publications to "tackle the weak spots" in the industries they cover, and Korman concurs. "I get in people's faces," he says. "People call us the bible of the construction industry."

The big reader response—25 letters poured in after the piece ran— validated the risk *ENR* took, though not all of the comments were supportive. One reader, capturing the two sides of the issue, wrote, "I, too, feel that the science of scheduling has changed immensely and the younger generation is leading toward developing instruction sheets rather than project measuring tools....Times have changed, however, and veteran consultants need to change."

Ockman, one of the original sources for the piece, wasn't completely happy, saying he wished Korman hadn't "put such a controversial spin" on the subject. In contrast, Wickwire, one of the other sources, was enthusiastic: "(The article) reverberated across the industry," he said.

In the end, the piece had an impact: the controversy became a topic at a 2004 conference hosted by the Association for the Advancement of Cost Engineering (where a panel moderator called the article the best thing that happened to the industry in 20 years) and the College of Scheduling at the Project Management Institute used the article as the kick-off for developing CPM scheduling guidelines.

Most important, though, was the change that came in software design. After the article ran, an engineering firm that had been using its own, proprietary scheduling software, switched to the main software at issue but only after modifying it to address many of the controversial features. Then, in 2005, that main software company integrated those modified features into its newest version, moving the software closer to the original intention of CPM scheduling.

—Michelle Vanderhoff

Project Management

Critics Can't Find the Logic in Many of Today's CPM Schedules

Users want software with flexibility, but is it true CPM?

By Richard Korman with Stephen H. Daniels

Four scheduling experts, all deeply experienced in the critical path method (CPM) that uses math to draw network diagrams of a project schedule, met recently in a restaurant just outside Philadelphia. The purpose was to discuss a new unit at the Project Management Institute, in Newtown Square, Pa. The College of Scheduling they have launched would promote "the fundamentals of project management" and encourage "a free exchange of ideas."

One of the reasons for starting the college is disconcerting. What is described as a CPM schedule these days sometimes isn't one at all, the four experts claim. If that claim is true, it says a lot about how personal computers have transformed scheduling and what could be in store as technology reshapes other phases of the construction process.

At the meeting, the four experts lamented the state of scheduling. They say they see widespread abuses of powerful software to produce badly flawed or deliberately deceptive schedules that look good but lack mathematical coherence or common sense about the way the industry works. The result is confusion, delayed projects and lawsuits.

How did this happen? PCs have popularized and democratized

74

CPM schedule writing, which first took hold in construction in the early 1960s, but it has also put scheduling in the hands of many inexperienced and poorly trained practitioners. When they do the work, critics say the basic principals of CPM are sometimes neglected or watered down.

The four men, three of whom are directors of PMI's College of Scheduling, reserved some of their most pointed comments for Primavera Systems Inc., the Bala Cynwyd, Pa.-based company that is the dominant supplier of construction project management and scheduling software. The four men say Primavera puts features in its popular scheduling programs that provide flexibility but are open to abuse.

Primavera's headquarters is about 10 miles from where the meeting took place and its president, Richard K. Faris, is active in industry affairs and is a board member of the new College of Scheduling. Significantly, he had not been invited to the meeting. Faris says the implication is dead wrong that Primavera can control the way its software is used. The company makes a robust and versatile product geared to the needs of its users, he says. Primavera can't be responsible for abuses any more than a spreadsheet company is responsible for those who use its product to draw up faulty or deceptive reports, he contends.

These critics "would like us to put in things that make people use the program in a certain way, but people don't want to buy a tool like that," says Faris, who founded the company with partner Joel Koppelman 20 years ago after they had both worked in the construction industry. "People want tools that are flexible, and if they are flexible they can be abused."

With annual sales of $77 million, 85 percent of it in scheduling software, Primavera is the biggest player in its market niche. Its P3 product, which sells for about $4,000 per concurrent license, is complemented by a simpler $500-per-user product called SureTrak. Competitors include Microsoft Corp., whose product is in the lower range. Meridian Project Systems also acquired technology in 2001 and began offering a CPM scheduling program.

With what it claims is 300,000 scheduling users around the world, Primavera is now answerable to a marketplace far wider than the handful of innovators at universities and corporate labs who gave birth to CPM scheduling. The software company also shapes the way the industry works through its popular product.

In its first decades, critical path method scheduling was the near-exclusive province of full-time project management consultants and construction managers. No longer. Thousands of contractors and many firms in other industries now are using low-cost scheduling software. Calculations that once needed mainframes routinely are performed on desktops.

To prevent errors by inexperienced users, one construction manager centralizes planning and scheduling within each company unit. "The new versions that are out are relatively inexpensive and relatively easy to learn, and that leads to the temptation to have relatively inexperienced people doing some of the scheduling," says Dennis K. Bryan, director of scheduling for St. Louis-based McCarthy Co. In doing the work, fundamentals of CPM can be ignored, he says.

"Scheduling has moved away from the priests of scheduling to the common man and there are less knowledgeable people doing it," says Faris. He says training is therefore vital.

Among the four critics who attended the Philadelphia meeting was at least one who qualifies as a scheduling priest. James J. O'Brien, an engineer and CPM pioneer, was the co-founder of O'Brien Kreitzberg (subsequently acquired by URS Corp.). The firm was the oldest and largest specializing in program and construction management. He was joined by Fredric L. Plotnick, an attorney, engineer and consultant who co-authored with O'Brien the latest edition of CPM in Construction Management (McGraw-Hill, 1999). The two other critics were Jon M. Wickwire, a Vienna, Va.-based attorney and consultant who has written extensively on CPM, and Stuart Ockman, a project management consultant based in Wallingford, Pa.

What they have seen they have sometimes described as rotten bananas in a software paradise: flawed schedules produced with powerful new tools.

In particular, the current method of CPM scheduling, Precedence Diagramming Method (PDM), which became the de facto standard in the U.S. in the mid-1990s, is open to manipulation and deception, they say. For example, PDM allows users to assign different calendars to different activities, which means if those activities are on the same logic path they won't show up with the same amount of float, the cushion of days in a schedule before a delay can hold up the entire job.

"That's like saying the grass is not green anymore to a classically trained scheduler from the 60s, 70s and maybe early 80s," says Ockman. Although he doesn't blame Primavera, he says, "The fact is that the primary de facto standard has prevented CPM from being practiced the way the inventors created it."

Faris answers that multiple calendars make scheduling more complicated but that users say they want them to match up with the different types of workweeks common today.

No Support

A turning point came in 1994, when Primavera switched the platform for its programs to the Windows operating system, which Microsoft uses. When it made the change, Primavera stopped supporting the Arrow Diagramming Method (ADM). Most users had already switched to drawing up their schedules using PDM.

O'Brien sent out an alarm to colleagues in 1997. "It appears that Primavera is trying (apparently with great success) to eradicate CPM as we know it," O'Brien wrote. Later, he added, "I have a sci-fi feeling that computers are being used to steal control of the art of planning and scheduling."

That feeling still lingers for O'Brien. "Some people want to wipe out the part of scheduling we grew up with, saying it's all software...you almost can't get a program on ADM, and it's frustrating," O'Brien says. As if to underscore the issue, the latest edition of O'Brien's book comes with a Primavera CD.

Under PDM, activities on a network diagram can be connected from either the activity's start or finish, and lag and lead factors can be used, allowing what some say is a cleaner, clearer diagram. But the logic behind the schedule then is not apparent on its face, as it is with ADM, and that's a step backward, says O'Brien.

Not everyone is displeased. "I think PDM is a much clearer representation of the logic of the schedule" and flow of work, says James L. Jenkins, assistant professor in the Dept. of Building Construction Management at Purdue University, West Lafayette, Ind. "You know exactly once you finish an activity which activities can start."

One possible disadvantage of PDM involves the display of the time that elapses before the next activity. With PDM's time-scaled display, the information can be hard to read, says Scott Kramer, associate professor in the Building Science Dept. at Auburn University, Auburn, Ala. With time-scaled PDM, the display can start to look like "a plate of spaghetti," and so people often suppress the logic arrows and use the easy-to-read bar chart. "That's what I like about Primavera," says Kramer, who teaches both ADM and PDM.

Nothing epitomizes the changes in CPM scheduling more than the reappearance of bar charts as graphic summaries of the schedules. For many schedule experts raised on ADM, the critical path can't be as readily identified in a bar chart, and its return is one of O'Brien's biggest disappointments. During the recent meeting, he picked up a hand-drawn ADM diagram, something that is little seen any more.

There are other concerns. Instead of being a trustworthy planning tool, some of the new schedules are minefields, say the critics. Wickwire and Plotnick are especially concerned about the options in the software to override or retain logic or impose or remove restraints. One of the problems they see in PDM is automatically making an activity or string of activities critical that may not belong on the critical path, a practice that they claim is anathema to well-trained CPM users.

"The point is, we lose the intellectual rigor and discipline required to properly go ahead and to properly utilize the technique," says Wickwire. A law book he co-authored, Construction Scheduling: Preparation, Liability, and Claims (Aspen Publishers, 2003), is full of examples of schedules being written or altered improperly. In one example from a few years ago, a contractor simply shortened the duration of activities in the later stages of a project when work fell behind on the early phases. But good scheduling practices require monthly updates including performing forward or backward passes through the entire project.

As for the software, all that's needed in some instances are asterisks to draw attention to places where the logic has been overridden, says Plotnick. "Its not the software's fault, but the software company should have something in there so the engineer is given a warning when somebody is misusing it," he says.

Faris agrees that leads and lags can be used excessively, but he says assigned constraints and retained logic both have legitimate uses.

One complaint by O'Brien and others is that polished, easy-to-read graphics are being emphasized over process integrity. That complaint, agrees Russell J. Lewton, construction manager for the Weitz Co. LLC, Des Moines, is right on target. "You must be careful not to be sucked in by the fact that it is a polished-looking schedule because computer schedules can be overwhelming (in size and complexity) when they incorporate too great a level of detail," he says. But if not sufficiently detailed, they are meaningless, he adds.

"Among the young guys, computers have made it easy to slap together something that looks right, but there is a thought process that must be involved, and it is hard to tell in many contemporary schedules if the thinking happened or not," Lewton says. Weitz puts the schedule writer together with the project staff to get "the right detail for the application."

Avoiding Clutter

A similar dilemma exists for other contractors. A "big and complicated" schedule negates its effectiveness, says Allen P. Read, chief scheduler for Salt Lake City-based Layton Construction Co. For that reason, he avoids resource loading, data on work crews and other things needed for the job, unless he must do so because a public works agency requires it. Some government agencies want to see a lot of specifications and milestones and some even limit the duration of project activities. As result, Read may have to break the activities into components, "adding clutter to the schedule."

Others say cooperation and how a schedule is prepared and used on the project is more important than errors by schedulers made possible by the software. "The most glaring weaknesses in schedules result from a failure to seek adequate buy-in at the front end," says Joe Wathan, a project director for San Mateo, Calif-based Webcor Builders. But he also says that the tools available in scheduling software are running ahead of the training and resources dedicated to using it. "If you take the Lamborghini scheduling tools on a large project without the resources necessary to manage the tool, we still get the student-driver result," he says.

Another phenomena worth noting, says Kent D. Pothast, scheduling manager for Portland, Ore.-based Hoffman Construction Co., is that schedules often are anticipated as tools in claims and lawsuits. As a result, what may have started as a pure construction schedule is written to include owner decisions, architect's timely submittal of drawings, approval processes for changes and other data. The common result, whether float is being added or eliminated, is "you are trying to keep somebody off you or put pressure on somebody else," says Pothast.

Some contractors set up schedules in which anyone else's delay of any kind allows them to file for more time and money. Government agencies are wising up, however. At least one agency now specifies how many activities can be within two weeks of the critical path to stop contractors from putting in semi-artificial activities to get rid of float, says Pothast.

The software programs all do the same thing, he says, and once activities, durations and logic are entered "you can trust the software," says Pothast.

Plotnick wants scheduling to be a branch of engineering, like steel design, so that software is used properly and those who would perpetrate deceptions can be penalized. Others say the only solution is to discourage questionable PDM practices, which is exactly why the College of Scheduling exists. O'Brien says he believes Primavera wants to do what's best for the industry and produces an excellent product. "Like the gun industry, their exceptional product can be put to bad purposes," he says.

Primavera's Faris questions whether the software firm has the responsibility to uphold law and order. His answer: "We have the responsibility to provide a tool that provides correct answers."

Reproduced with permission from the McGraw-Hill Companies, Inc.

JOURNALISM
THAT
MATTERS

Chapter 7

Second Thoughts on a Lobbying Plan

Exposed by Housing Affairs Letter, *a former U.S. official decides not to charge a fee for help on a rule he wrote*

Sometimes high-impact stories take months of investigation to uncover. For Tom Edwards, a veteran reporter for a specialty trade publication in Washington, D.C., *Housing Affairs Letter,* which covers government housing programs, a crucial tip fell into his lap—and he wasted no time in acting on it.

In mid-2005 a reader shared with Edwards a solicitation letter that was then circulating among top executives of public housing authorities (PHAs), the local governmental agencies that own and operate federally subsidized rental housing developments for low-income households.

Although these PHA executives receive solicitations all the time from vendors providing specialized services, this one was notable because of whom it was from: Michael Liu, a former assistant secretary of public housing in the U.S. Department of Housing and Urban Development. Also on the letter was Phil Musser, a former HUD chief of staff.

Less than a year earlier, Liu was the top federal official writing the rules and disbursing the funds that applied to these PHA executives. Now he was offering his assistance to these same people as a lobbyist with Dutko Worldwide. Was this a conflict of interest?

To be sure, federal officials parlay their government expertise into lucrative private practice all the time. This revolving door among experts in arcane legislative and regulatory areas is part of the very fiber of Washington and, by some accounts, integral for maintaining the expertise needed to properly oversee and advocate for complex programs.

To Edwards, though, this revolving door circled around a bit too quickly. Not only had Liu just left HUD before joining the lobbying firm, but while at the department he played an unusually significant role in creating the funding rules that the memo was now offering to help decipher.

Finding a Fair Funding Formula

Liu's letter came at the tail end of a multi-year saga for HUD as it tried to determine a fair formula for how public housing authorities around the country receive federal funding for covering their operating costs.

In 1998, Congress instructed HUD to develop rules and create a new formula for determining how to distribute funds to PHAs to save money and to ensure funding allocations are based on each authority's assets. Over the course of several years following the congressional mandate, HUD was unable to draft a formula and commissioned Harvard University to conduct a study. The resulting formula, in June 2003, was not received well by public housing agencies, because it would cause some agencies to lose money, so HUD and the PHA advocates then worked together to develop a working formula, completed a year later. But soon after, in March 2005, Liu made dramatic changes to the rules that, analysts believed, were intended to work in favor of HUD.

On April 30, 2005, within weeks of signing off on the rule changes, Liu left the department. Three days later, he joined Dutko to head up its housing practice as a senior vice president; Musser was hired as a vice president in July.

A short time afterward, Liu and Musser sent the memo on Dutko letterhead soliciting public housing authorities to commit to four- and five-figure fees to have Dutko represent them in negotiating for funds from HUD under the new rules. Under their plan, Dutko would launch a group called the Coalition for Fairness that would protect the interests of public housing authorities and ensure the rules are executed as negotiated. To join, housing authorities would pay up to several thousand dollars a month for the duration of the coalition, with the amount based on the size of the PHA. Essentially, it appeared as if Liu was trying to cash in on lobbying assignments directly related to rules he finalized a few months earlier while at HUD.

"Using information on HUD to further your career on the outside is a little questionable," Edwards says. "Particularly if you were going to use something that you in fact altered in the process and then came back and told people that you would help them decipher the same problems you helped create. That was a red flag to me."

Edwards knew he had not only a breaking story, but one with implications directly impacting his readers, many of whom had likely received the memo and might have been considering signing on.

Edwards' first step was to verify the legitimacy of the memo. Calls to Liu, Musser, and Dutko were not returned, but he confirmed with several other sources that they too had received the same document from the lobbying firm. His second step was to piece together the sequence of events culminating with Liu's resignation and his launch of the lobbying effort.

Housing Affairs *Letter*

THE INDEPENDENT WEEKLY WASHINGTON REPORT ON HOUSING

Housing Affairs Letter

www.cdpublications.com/pubs/housingaffairsletter.php

Established: 1961

Publisher: CD Publications, Silver Spring, Md.

Frequency: Weekly

Characteristics: Newsletter, 8 pages

Circulation: Not available

Readership: Officials at the U.S. Department of Housing and Urban Development, local government housing officials, and members of the housing industry's private sector

Editorial staff: Editor and an associate editor

The first of two articles Edwards wrote ran in the August 19 issue of *Housing Affairs Letter*, outlining the memo and explaining the implications and apparent conflict of interest. In a follow-up article a week later, Edwards reported that the newsletter's first article set into motion questions among public housing authorities and HUD, and that the lobbying plan designed by Liu was in jeopardy.

The second article also explained that, in addition to the ethical questions, Liu's actions may have been in violation of the Byrd Amendment, which prohibits the use of federal "contract, grant, loan, or cooperative agreement funds to pay any person for influencing or attempting to influence the executive or legislative branch with respect to certain specified actions," as well as the 1995 Lobbying Disclosure Act, which prohibits lobbying former colleagues for a year.

Joe Haas, managing editor of CD Publications, which publishes *Housing Affairs Letter*, said the articles sent Dutko backpedaling in its decision to solicit fees from the public housing groups. Additional pressure began to build after CD Publications distributed a press release about the articles to more than a dozen media outlets and the story was picked up Sept. 1 by *The Washington Post*, which ran a brief in its "Special Interests" column on The Federal Page, an inside-the-beltway favorite among lobbyists.

In the *Post* piece, called "A Lobbying Venture stymied," Liu announced he wouldn't move forward with the lobbying after all, saying he had other things to do. "There won't be a coalition," he told the *Post*. "We're too busy to attempt to pursue this." Liu also acknowledged the awkwardness created by the timing issues.

Liu, wrote *Post* reporter Judy Sarasohn, "acknowledged that he would have had to work behind the scenes on the effort because of restrictions on his ability to lobby HUD as a result of his involvement with the operating-subsidy formula and the rule." The one-year lobbying restriction on Musser was already over.

Edwards says the response from his readers—many of whom had received the memo and were outraged when they found out about the back story behind it—was more than any article he's done before.

"Breaking a story I think proves value to the readers," says Edwards.

And "when it's directly tied into a program, as in this case, that is of direct interest to a good portion of your publication's readers, I think that only makes it even more valuable," says Haas. "It's one thing to do some muckraking, but when the muckraking also affects the reader's bottom line, even more value is provided."

Haas says he was not worried about ramifications of the story because of the trust he has in Edwards to ensure factual correctness and because he confirmed the existence of the memo and its implications. The company's editorial independence also helps avoid any taint of favoritism or partisanship.

"Any time a publication can break a story like that, it seems a really good opportunity," says Haas, "both to break an important story but also to demonstrate that your publication is capable of getting out ahead and finding a story that nobody else has."

—*Katy Tomasulo*

Public Housing

Cashing In on Neg Reg

By Tom Edwards

Two former senior HUD officials, now lobbyists in the private sector, have organized a new lobby for public housing authorities anticipating a financial windfall under the new public-housing operating formula.

A solicitation memo—with former HUD Assistant Secy. for Public & Indian Housing Michael Liu and former HUD Chief-of-Staff Philip Musser as the lobby contacts—has been obtained by HAL.

The memo is on Dutko World Wide letterhead. Dutko bills itself as a multidisciplinary strategy and management firm. A call by HAL to Liu and/or Musser to discuss the venture was not returned.

Public-housing advocates are stung by the implication they don't have a grasp of the issue. They see the effort as a device for Liu to cash in on a regulation he had a direct hand in developing last year.

Liu subsequently gutted the negotiated formula in a proposed rule published in April, two weeks before he departed HUD and joined Dutko.

In the interim, appropriators in both houses of Congress have rejected Liu's changes and demand HUD abide by the original negotiated formula. The admonition is expected to be included in the final report accompanying the FY 2006 HUD appropriation bill.

Liu and Musser—he joined Dutko in July 2004—use congressional support of the original negotiated rule as their main selling point to PHAs, although they allude to the proposed rule as well.

Only PHAs which receive an operating-fund increase under the June 2004 formula and the April 2005 proposed rule are eligible for membership in the "Coalition for Fairness," otherwise billed in the memo as the "operating subsidy coalition."

"The Coalition is dedicated to protecting the interests of PHAs that gain under the negotiated or proposed rule and to ensure to the extent possible that the rule as negotiated is executed," the memo asserts.

Playing on the assumption present public-housing lobbies are not capable of adequately representing their clients on the single issue, Dutko reminds PHAs House appropriators added $200 million to FY 2006 operating-fund appropriations and claims the firm would be the organization "in Washington that only represents the interest of PHAs that gain under the new rule and that would get a 'seat at the table' as potential points of compromise develop."

A six-month membership in the enterprise comes at a price—$1,000 a month or $5,000 upfront for small PHAs, $2,000 a month or $10,000 upfront for medium-size PHAs, and $4,000 a month or $20,000 upfront for large agencies.

The lobby says it needs commitments from about 20 PHAs to get underway and a membership base of 30-40 PHAs to make it work. In return, member PHAs would get a bimonthly e-mail newsletter and a monthly conference call along with the lobbying efforts. How federal rules governing former government officials lobbying their peers remain to be seen.

Additional inducements include a warning present legislative language doesn't describe how the operating fund will be distributed if the formula can't be funded at 100% and a reminder the Senate didn't follow the House lead adding money to operations.

Another magnet is the $50 million set-aside for transitional costs for those PHAs not receiving an increase. Dutko claims in the memo PHAs gaining operating money should be eligible for transitional money as well because many will incur "extraordinary costs."

Dutko says its guiding principle for all decisions "will be based on whether or not an issue advances the cause of implementing the operating subsidy rule as negotiated." The firm adds it will urge Congress to implement the increased subsidies fully for FY 2006 and call for across-the-board transition aid.

The controversy over Liu's unilateral alteration of the operating-subsidy formula erupted with Federal Register publication of a proposed rule April 14.

Liu had signed off on the rule change March 18, at a time he knew of his impending April 30 departure. How Liu's decision then influenced his plan to develop a lobbying strategy later is not explained.

But HUD was apparently miffed over housing-advocate pressure on Congress to abide by its mandate for negotiated rulemaking after HUD attempted to sidestep the mandate and push through a rule on its own.

Sources told HAL at the time HUD senior executives were furious at being forced by Congress to conduct four often acrimonious sessions over 10 hours, and the subsequent change was retaliation against the housing lobbies.

Congress first mandated creation of a new formula in 1998 and told HUD to negotiate a rule instead of issuing one unilaterally. HUD complained it didn't have sufficient background information to proceed and persuaded Congress to provide $3 million for a three-year study by the Harvard Graduate School of Design, effectively delaying the process.

The study, unveiled in 2003, was opposed by advocates who considered it flawed because it compared public housing operating costs to those in the private sector.

HUD rejected an offer from advocates to negotiate, forcing Congress' hand. Congress told HUD in the FY 2004 Consolidated Appropriations Act to abide by its mandate to negotiate.

Reproduced with permission from CD Publications.

JOURNALISM
THAT
MATTERS

Chapter 8

Not Worth the Paper it's Printed On

The U.S. government weeds out bogus degree-holders in its midst after
Government Computer News *uncovers an egregious example of*
resume padding

In 2003, when U.S. Senator Susan Collins (R-Maine) and Rep. Tom Davis (R-Va.) initiated a federal investigation into diploma mills—the unaccredited institutions that award university degrees for little more than a fee, an essay, and a wink—they pointed to the egregious example of Laura Callahan.

With her Ph.D. in computer information science, the former deputy chief information officer at the U.S. departments of Labor and Homeland Security had every appearance of being the kind of academic heavyweight appropriate for such high level jobs. But her alma mater, Hamilton University, is just a dusty former motel in Evanston, Wyo., something that came to the lawmakers' attention after the publication I write for, *Government Computer News*, broke the story on its Web site in a May 30, 2003, piece, and spurred a spurt of coverage by the national consumer media.

The U.S. Office of Personnel Management, which functions as the federal government's human resources department, has since instituted changes to the way it looks into educational claims made on federal job application forms. Among other things, it's added a system for categorizing academic institutions as either conventional/accredited, non-accredited/pending accreditation, or non-accredited. The changes, says Stephen Benowitz, OPM associate director for human resources prod-

88

ucts and services, are intended to clarify "when and what education will satisfy requirements for qualifications and training." Benowitz made his remarks at hearing hosted by Sen. Collins' committee in 2004.

Anonymous Tip

Our story lead came through an anonymous tip.

In March 2002, as the U.S. Department of Homeland Security was just beginning to take shape, the source made me aware of Callahan and Hamilton University and gave me supporting documents that included the application materials from the school.

In reviewing the material with others at the publication, it became clear that Callahan bought more than just her Ph.D. from the school; her B.A. and M.A. were bought from there, too.

Within days of our initial coverage, which I wrote for the GCN Web site with a colleague, Wilson Dizard III, Callahan was suspended by her department (with pay), while departmental officials checked out the story. She resigned a year later, after pursuing all the administrative appeals available.

Following that, Dizard and I researched how many other federal employees might also have used fake degrees from unaccredited schools to inflate their credentials. Using a database of diploma mills established by the Oregon government, through its aptly named Office of Degree Authorization, we screened hundreds of IT professionals in the government, and found dozens of

Government Computer News

www.gcn.com

Established: 1982

Publisher: Post Newsweek Tech Media

Frequency: 34 issues per year

Characteristics: Four-color, average 60 tabloid pages per issue

Circulation: 100,000 controlled, qualified

Readership: Government information technology officers and specialists

Editorial staff: Editor-in-chief, editorial director, managing editor, assistant managing editor-online, assistant managing editor-technology, senior technology analyst, senior writer, associate writer, technology analyst, assistant managing editor-news, 3 senior writers, 2 staff writers, assistant managing editor-features, senior writer-features, 3 copy editors, editorial support

people claiming bogus degrees. Among these people were some presidential appointees.

The issue of diploma mills soon took on a life of its own, with the federal government and others in the media following up with their own investigations. Callahan appeared on *60 Minutes II* to defend herself, claiming to have been duped by the school. Meanwhile, the fallout continues to be felt today as federal and other job applicants get their academic claims scrutinized with a fine-toothed comb.

—*Patience Wait*

HSD Official Obtained Ph.D. From Diploma Mill

By Patience Wait and Wilson P. Dizard III

A high-ranking career official in the Homeland Security Department apparently obtained her doctorate from a Wyoming diploma mill.

Laura L. Callahan, now senior director in the office of department CIO Steven Cooper, states on her professional biography that she "holds a Ph.D. in Computer Information Systems from Hamilton University." Callahan, who is also president of the Association for Federal IRM and a member of the CIO Council, is commonly called by the title "Dr."

Callahan's resume says she began her civil service career in 1984. Before joining HSD, she was deputy CIO at the Labor Department.

Hamilton University, according to an Internet search, is located in Evanston, Wyo. It is affiliated with and supported by Faith in the Order of Nature Fellowship Church, also in Evanston. The state of Wyoming does not license Hamilton because it claims a religious exemption. Oregon has identified Hamilton University as a diploma mill unaccredited by any organization recognized by the U.S. Department of Education.

Callahan could not be reached for comment after repeated calls to her office. Michelle Petrovich, a department spokeswoman, said Friday afternoon, "We have no reason at this time not to believe Laura Callahan's credentials, and we will look into the matter." On Monday, officials were continuing their investigation, she said.

The department's CIO, Steve Cooper, also did not return repeated calls seeking comment.

Diploma mills and their potential for fraud were the subject of an inquiry by the General Accounting Office at the request of Sen. Susan M. Collins (R-Maine), who now chairs the Senate Governmental Affairs Committee. In a November 2002 report, GAO described how it purchased bachelor's and master's degrees in Collins' name from Degrees-R-Us of Las Vegas. It referred the matter to the Federal Trade Commission. An aide to Collins on Monday said the senator would have a comment later in the week.

Andrew O'Connell of GAO's Office of Special Investigations said of any government employee who purchases a fake diploma, "There's no doubt in our mind that it's a scam on the government."

A search of accredited institutions turned up four colleges and universities with the name Hamilton, in addition to Hamilton University: Hamilton College in Clinton, N.Y.; Hamilton College in Cedar Rapids, Iowa; Hamilton Technical College in Davenport, Iowa; and Suwannee-Hamilton Technical Center in Live Oak, Fla. None of the four awards doctoral degrees.

In its printed materials, Hamilton University lists the National Park Service among organizations that employ its degree-holders, or that reimbursed employees who obtained Hamilton degrees.

Hamilton's material said it provides degrees to individuals who state that their life and work experiences give them qualifications comparable to those of persons who complete academic courses and theses or dissertations to obtain degrees. The bulk of communications between Hamilton and its customers is via e-mails, faxes and postal mail. Calls to Hamilton go to a voice-mail system.

"They bought an old motel and took it apart and furnished it with stucco. It's very nice," said Connie Morris, executive assistant at the Evanston, Wyo., Chamber of Commerce. "They are members of the Chamber. They have two or three employees."

The Oregon Office of Degree Authorization quotes Webster's Third New International Dictionary on the definition of a diploma mill: An institution of higher education operating without supervision of a state or professional agency and granting diplomas which are either fraudulent or because of the lack of proper standards worthless.

According to a spokesman for the Office of Personnel

Management, the penalties for providing false or misleading information, including submitting false academic credentials, include termination or other serious disciplinary actions.

"There is no regulation that addresses diploma mills. You are talking about falsification of academic credentials," the OPM spokesman said.

Lawrence Lorber, a partner with the Washington law firm Proskauer Rose LLP who specializes in labor and employment law, spoke with a reporter about circumstances matching Callahan's claim to a Ph.D., though he specifically asked not to be told of the person or federal departments involved.

"There is something called resume fraud, which this would be considered," Lorber said. "It's what it sounds like—not the embellishment, but a fraudulent addition that indicates a job or degree."

It is the accreditation of the program—or lack thereof—that becomes important, Lorber said. "By listing it [on your resume] you are creating the presumption that it's from an accredited, recognized institution."

Hamilton University's enrollment application and enrollment invitation spell out the simple requirements for students who wish to obtain a Ph.D.

■ $3,600, payable up front by bank draft or personal check only. Hamilton does not accept credit cards.

■ Completing one course at home on "personal, business and professional ethics." Hamilton provides the course workbook, and the student must complete the open-book examination that is included. The school's materials state the course and test require an average of five to eight hours to complete.

■ Writing one paper relevant to the area in which the Ph.D. is being sought. The minimum length for the paper is 2,000 words, or roughly four pages, and will "be referred to as a dissertation," the materials say.

In return, Hamilton promises to deliver "an official diploma in a leather bound holder… of the highest possible quality and carry[ing] the official raised seal of the university." The organization promises that the "diplomas granted by Hamilton University do not reflect how the degree requirements were met (traditionally or externally)."

Because prospective employers often want to verify a candidate's education, Hamilton also promises to provide verification of degrees, once the person provides authorization to release the information.

In this case, for instance, when asked via e-mail to verify Callahan's Ph.D., the registrar's office of Hamilton University replied, "All requests for degree verification must be made in writing and must be accompanied by an authorization signed by the graduate."

But Hamilton promises that when it provides transcripts, they will look like real transcripts, even providing numbers, titles and grades for courses the student did not take, because their requirement was waived due to life or work experience. The transcripts will not say the courses were waived, and the grade average shown for an entire transcript will be based on the grades for the at-home test and the dissertation.

A person identifying himself as Dr. R.G. Marn, faculty adviser, said the institution's privacy policies prevented it from releasing records. He declined to comment on whether Hamilton University is a diploma mill.

Reproduced with permission from Post Newsweek Tech Media.

JOURNALISM
THAT
MATTERS

Chapter 9

When U.S.-Canada Tax Relations Hang in the Balance

Transfer Pricing Report helps the two countries agree to stop bickering on trans-border tax issues

In light of hot spots like Iraq and North Korea, Americans don't lie awake at night worrying about conflicts between the United States and Canada. But for those of us in the world of international tax, strained relations between the two countries has become a very real problem in recent years. A story I wrote in September 2004 for BNA's *Transfer Pricing Report* helped identify the causes of the conflict and prodded officials at the highest levels of government to begin working out their differences.

When a company has operations in more than one country, disputes often arise among revenue agencies over the amount of income earned—and thus subject to taxation—in each country. Most countries' tax agencies, including the Internal Revenue Service and its Canadian equivalent, the Canada Revenue Agency (CRA), have offices called "competent authorities" that are dedicated to resolving those disputes. Through negotiation, the competent authorities make sure companies aren't taxed more than once on the same income—or, in rare cases where double tax occurs, they try to minimize the amount.

Months before I wrote the story, I'd been hearing complaints even from my most reticent government sources about how difficult negotiations had become between the U.S. and Canadian competent authority offices. U.S. government officials aren't supposed to discuss their dealings with any particular foreign country, but some of them had called me on background to say that Canadian officials were taking extreme negotiating positions. It was rumored that higher-ups in the CRA were encouraging auditors to maximize Canadian tax regardless of whether this caused double tax for the companies.

After calling around, I got a tip that some companies were so frustrated with the situation that they were threatening to take their cases to court in Canada—a much more expensive and contentious route than going through the competent authority. One source even told me some U.S. government officials were so frustrated with the situation in Canada that they weren't trying to dissuade the companies from going to court.

The threat of litigation, together with background from U.S. government officials, gave me the news peg I needed. The challenge would be finding someone to go on the record with the complaints. Most people were reluctant to say anything too negative because they had U.S.-Canada cases pending for competent authority review and didn't want to poison the negotiations. On a suggestion from one source, however, I called Judy Scarabello, vice president for tax policy at the National Foreign Trade Council. Since her organization represents the interests of U.S. multinational companies as a whole, she was in a position to relay complaints about Canada from a number of companies without endangering the interests of any one of them.

More Research

Scarabello's comments would have given me enough for a short news story, but they didn't explain how U.S.-Canada negotiations had become so contentious. They also didn't give the Canadian side of the story. To make sure the article was balanced, I interviewed additional practitioners in the international tax area, many of them current or former government tax officials. Ten of those quoted in the story— nine by name, one anonymously—practiced in the United States, and seven—including one unnamed government spokeswoman—were Canadian.

Former officials from both countries who had presided over negotiations in better times provided historical perspective. Some, including Claude Lemelin, who a decade before had been Canada's chief transfer pricing official, said negotiations tend to go better when fewer people are involved. He and others noted that both countries' competent

Transfer Pricing Report

www.bnatax.com/tm/trans-
ferpricing_details.htm

Established: 1991

Publisher: Bureau of
National Affairs,
Washington, D.C.

Frequency: Bi-weekly

Characteristics: Newsletter,
average 48 pages

Circulation: Not available

Readership: Transfer pricing
advisors, corporate and public tax officials

Editorial staff: Managing
editor, 2 full-time and 1
part-time editor/reporter

authority offices had expanded significantly over the years. With growth, successful results were more likely to come
from principled negotiating rather than
deal making—not always an easy transition.

One attorney, Steven Wrappe of
Deloitte Tax, said plant closings under the
North American Free Trade Agreement
likely compounded the problem. Under
NAFTA, he said, a number of plants that
were struggling to maintain operations
in one country closed and the work
moved to the plant in the other country.
When that happened, the surviving plant
had to compensate the one that closed.
These compensation calculations were
difficult and in many cases the tax
authorities, unable to agree in principle,
reached a compromise that left both sides
unsatisfied. At that point, "the seeds of
discontent are sown," Wrappe said.

Others I interviewed pointed to the
uneven relationship between the two
countries as a possible source of stress.
Most Canadian multinational interests
are subsidiaries, not parents, of U.S. companies. Some kinds of economic analysis
tend to produce more revenue in the parent company, while others tend to attribute more income to the subsidiary.
Accordingly, U.S. auditors were favoring one analysis and Canadian
auditors another.

A separate problem was U.S. officials' reluctance to visit a company's business along with their Canadian counterparts in a type of
negotiation called an advance pricing agreement, or APA. Both the
United States and Canada (and most of their major trading partners)
allow for APAs, in which a multinational company and the tax agencies
involved work out how to allocate income among the countries for
future years' taxation. When these negotiations required a trip to the

company's location, Canadian officials preferred to conduct the visit with officials representing the other country "to ensure that both sides receive the same information and facts at the same time," according to a spokeswoman from the CRA. The head of the U.S. APA program, however, said he had not found these joint visits especially useful.

Impact

The approximately 5,000-word story that came out in September 2004, "As Negotiations Falter, U.S. Competent Authority 'Not Discouraging' Litigation in Canadian Courts," told the tale of conflict between the two countries in much the way I've laid it out here. I knew it would cause some heartburn at both taxing agencies, particularly the CRA, but I had no idea how big an impact it would ultimately have.

In late October of 2004, about a month after the story broke, a Canadian official said publicly that the U.S. and Canada were working toward agreement on one of the disputed issues I had mentioned in my article. In March, Costco, the big box retailer, announced a settlement with the U.S. and Canadian tax agencies eliminating all double tax for 1996-2003. In addition, several people told me the three most recent rounds of U.S.-Canada competent authority negotiations, in January, March, and June of 2005, had gone exceptionally well, with a number of long-stalled cases moving forward. I covered each of these developments, but perhaps the most gratifying, concrete evidence of the story's impact were three memoranda of understanding signed by Robert Green, the head of the U.S. competent authority office, and his Canadian counterpart, Fred O'Riordan, stating that the two nations would strive for reciprocal and consistent treatment of tax issues and setting out procedures for resolving stalled cases.

A former U.S. Treasury official, Charles Triplett of Mayer, Brown, Rowe & Maw, called my article "an excellent piece of investigative journalism that is rarely seen in such specialized areas as international taxation" and said the story was a "catalyst" in drawing attention to the problems between the countries. For those of us writing about very technical areas, the opportunity to make a change for the better can be elusive. I treasure the compliment.

—Molly Moses

Feature Report

As Negotiations Falter, U.S. Competent Authority 'Not Discouraging' Litigation in Canadian Courts

By Molly Moses

As competent authority negotiations between the United States and Canada continue to deteriorate, taxpayers increasingly are threatening to resolve their double tax disputes through litigation in Canadian courts—with tacit approval from frustrated U.S. negotiators.

While practitioners blamed both countries' tax authorities for the decline of the U.S.-Canada relationship, which many said was at an all-time low, the more severe criticisms were leveled at the Canada Revenue Agency. Sources accused the CRA of taking inconsistent positions designed to maximize Canadian revenue in every case, disallowing deductions for intangibles routinely permitted by other tax authorities, and failing to negotiate in good faith.

The Internal Revenue Service, meanwhile, drew criticism for a lack of flexibility, a tendency to undervalue Canadian subsidiaries' contributions to intangibles, and for failing, in advance pricing agreement negotiations, to see the merit of bilateral visits to a taxpayer site.

Judy Scarabello, Vice President for Tax Policy at the National Foreign Trade Council, contended the CRA's revenue-driven approach was responsible for the stalled competent authority cases. She argued Canada is unjustifiably eliminating deductions other countries allow, and that "because companies can't get through the competent authority process in Canada—Canada either won't come to the table, or if it does, won't concede any of the adjustments—some taxpayers are threatening to litigate." Moreover, Scarabello added, the approach is getting results. Companies going to court, she said, "have been getting a little bit better treatment and allowed more of a deduction."

Scarabello further asserted that the U.S. Competent Authority currently has so little faith in its ability to resolve cases with the

CRA that it is not discouraging taxpayers from taking their transfer pricing cases to court in Canada—an assertion IRS Director, International Robert Green would "neither confirm nor deny."

Francois Vincent of KPMG in Montreal wrote in August about increased transfer pricing activity in the Tax Court of Canada, with two recent cases involving U.S. taxpayers. *Canada Safeway Ltd. v. The Queen*, Can. T.C., No. 2003-2925(IT)G, filed in August 2003, involves transactions between the Canadian subsidiary of U.S. grocery retailer Safeway Inc. and another Safeway subsidiary located in the United States, while *Norand Data Systems Ltd. v. The Queen*, Can. T.C., No. 2003- 3525(IT)G, filed in October 2003, concerns a corporation in the United States carrying on business in Canada through a permanent establishment (13 *Transfer Pricing Report* 460, 8/18/04).

Since Canada is the United States' largest trading partner, a breakdown in competent authority negotiations is a serious problem. Deputy U.S. Treasury International Tax Counsel Patricia Brown said Sept. 3 that the U.S. Competent Authority is negotiating about 200 cases with 36 countries. Only 20 percent of cases filed in 2003 resulted from U.S. adjustments, and 40 percent of the entire case load was with Canada, she told a meeting of the International Fiscal Association in Salzburg (13 *Transfer Pricing Report* 467, 9/15/04).

The NAFTA Factor

Steven Wrappe of Deloitte & Touche LLP in Washington, D.C., said the plant closings that occurred in both Canada and the United States following implementation of the North American Free Trade Agreement in 1994 may have contributed to some of the tension between the two governments. Before NAFTA—which was designed to remove barriers to trade and investment among the United States, Canada, and Mexico—a company might have had manufacturing plants in the United States and Canada that, with the economy at the time, were operating at about 50 percent of capacity, Wrappe said.

After NAFTA, the plant in one jurisdiction likely would have closed and the work would have moved to the plant in the other country. "Unrelated parties in this situation would continue to struggle on as long as they were able to cover the cost of the building," Wrappe said. "But with related parties, if you have two plants and you could close one and make the other very profitable, you would do it," he said. "The question then becomes how to compensate the closed plant."

Calculating the compensation "was a difficult exercise and also a very subjective activity, which often led to disputes" between the two countries, and much speculation arose on both sides about how unrelated parties would compensate the closed plant, Wrappe said. In many cases the tax authorities, unable to agree in principle, simply reached a compromise. When that happens, he said, both sides leave unsatisfied—and "the seeds of discontent are sown."

Size Matters

Some said the expansion of the APA and competent authority offices on both sides of the border also may have caused negotiations to falter.

Robert Kirschenbaum of Baker & McKenzie in Palo Alto, Calif., said that both the IRS APA Program and the Canadian Competent Authority experienced significant changes in personnel between 2000 and 2001, a time when their case loads dramatically increased. Three Canadian officials—Gary Zed, Deputy Director General of the International Tax Directorate; Sandra Goldberg, a senior official who worked on transfer pricing and competent authority issues; and John Oatway, an international tax official with Canada's transfer pricing division who was responsible for all aspects relating to transfer pricing policy and legislative matters—all left the government in late 2000 (9 *Transfer Pricing Report* 569, 12/13/00).

At the same time, in the United States, then-APA Program Director Sean Foley received approval to nearly double the size of the U.S. program (9 *Transfer Pricing Report* 416, 11/15/00).

Claude Lemelin, former chief of the transfer pricing section in Canada's International Tax Programs Directorate, said that "negotiating probably is a little bit easier when the program is not too big."

Lemelin, who left the government to join Price Waterhouse in Montreal in 1996, said that in 1995 there were roughly 12 to 15 people on the Canadian side dealing with APAs and competent authority cases. Now, he said, the Canadian Competent Authority has three full sections with six to seven people in each section. "In the early days as well the same group would provide advice to the Field," he said. Now a separate unit has that function. That unit as well has three sections, with eight or nine people in each section, Lemelin said.

Oatway, now with Deloitte & Touche LLP in Ottawa, said that "in the late 1980s, there were three or four people in the Canadian Competent Authority that dealt with U.S.-Canada cases, and they had a good relationship with the U.S. people." At the time, there was more "deal making," he said.

Wrappe said that as both countries' APA and competent authority units grew, they had to rely less on deal making and more on principled negotiating, and also had to strive harder to achieve uniformity. "They had to evolve from a program of individuals to a program of rules for negotiating behavior," he said. "It's easy to have uniformity when you have three people, but it's harder with 30."

Personality clashes could be part of the problem in U.S.-Canada negotiations, other practitioners said. Robert Ackerman of Ernst & Young LLP, who was director of the U.S. APA Program from 1991 to 1994, said that "in the last three to four years, it would appear from my personal experience that the working relationships have become tense and, in certain cases, personal."

Ron Holowka of Ernst & Young LLP in Ottawa, coordinator of Canada's APA Program from July 1993 to August 2001, said he used to lecture his staff on the importance of maintaining cordial relations with negotiators on the other side. "It's not like buying a used car, where you're only going to see the person once," he said. "This is a relationship you need to preserve."

Reliance on Economists

Both the IRS and the CRA have come to rely more heavily on economists for international audits and competent authority matters over the years. A CRA spokeswoman said the agency had one economist in 1994 and now has 16, all of whom work at CRA headquarters. Eight economists work in the International Tax Operations Division, providing economic support to the Field, and the other eight work in the Competent Authority Services Division, providing economic analysis for mutual agreement procedure cases and APAs, she said.

Foley in August 2000 said he planned to increase the ratio of economists to attorneys in the U.S. APA Program, and the IRS in April 2003 confirmed the hiring of six Field economists, bringing the total number of IRS economists to 78 (9 *Transfer Pricing Report* 223, 8/9/00; 11 *Transfer Pricing Report* 1118, 4/30/03).

Canadian practitioners said in May that the introduction of economists has caused CRA officials to harden their positions during a transfer pricing audit, making it more difficult to resolve disputes, and that the CRA was mimicking the IRS in relying more on the experts (13 *Transfer Pricing Report* 63, 5/26/04).

Uneven Relationship

Phil West of Steptoe & Johnson LLP in Washington, D.C., said a natural tension exists between the United States and Canada because "we have so much trade with Canada but our economy is so much larger. . . . It's a unique relationship."

Robert Turner of Ernst & Young in Toronto pointed out an important difference in the dealings between the United Kingdom and the United States—which are relatively free of conflict—and Canada and the United States: cross investment. More of this occurs between the United States and the United Kingdom, while U.S.-Canada investment overwhelmingly consists of U.S. parent companies with Canadian subsidiaries, he said.

Oatway said the uneven relationship influenced how the tax authorities evaluated particular transactions. For example, in calculating the return for a stripped manufacturer in Canada, CRA officials would favor using full-fledged manufacturers as comparables and would adjust downward for the risks associated with carrying the inventory. The United States, on the other hand, likely would work on a cost plus basis, taking a lower cost base and adjusting upward. "The Canadian number would be higher—a product of the fact that Canada is a subsidiary country," Oatway said.

Patricia Lewis of Caplin & Drysdale in Washington, D.C., added that Canada "takes an expansive view of the intangibles that belong to a Canadian distributor or manufacturer if its functions are stripped out."

However, Brian Cromwell of The Ballentine Barbera Group in Palo Alto, Calif., said he had seen both of the approaches Oatway described applied in the United States, with sales and marketing service providers used as comparables under the cost plus method (12 *Transfer Pricing Report* 559, 10/15/03).

Others said Canada was not alone in challenging low returns to stripped entities. Lemelin noted that tax authorities in Europe are paying particular attention to commissionaire structures.

Intangibles

Overall, practitioners said intangibles cases—often the most contentious disputes between any two countries—were particularly hard for Canada and the United States to resolve, with the tax authorities far apart on the amount of royalties due a U.S. company from its Canadian subsidiary.

Martin Przysuski of BDO Dunwoody LLP in Markham, Ontario, said a U.S. company may charge royalties to a Canadian subsidiary that was "already well established in Canada for a number of decades." In such a case, he said, the CRA likely would oppose the royalty payment, arguing the Canadian subsidiary was the owner of the intangible by virtue of its activities in the Canadian market. Instead, the CRA may choose to allow the reimbursement of costs for specific value added services performed by the U.S. entity for the benefit of the Canadian subsidiary, Przysuski said. The cost deductions allowed by Canadian competent authority officials, however, could have been incurred for activities the U.S. parent claimed were related to the development of the intangible. "Therefore, back and forth ensues as to whether the activities contribute to the development of an intangible for which a royalty payment is due or services for which cost reimbursements are more appropriate," he said.

Another practitioner said the United States may have laid the groundwork for Canada's current position on marketing intangibles by taking the same position in competent authority cases negotiated 10 years ago.

KPMG's Vincent said the United States introduced the concept of marketing intangibles in competent authority and APA negotiations in the early 1990s. "Based on the 'cheese examples' in Regs. §1.482-4(f)(3), the U.S. government took the position, in a case involving a Canadian parent and a U.S. distributor, that the royalties from the distributor to the parent for the parent's intangibles should be reduced or eliminated as compensation for the distributor's efforts to develop and enhance those intangibles in the United States," Vincent said. "There are many more U.S. multinationals with distributors outside the United States, but no one had their eye on that at the time," he said. "In the mid-1990s, some Canadian Competent Authority analysts began to use the cheese examples argument in the reverse case of a Canadian distributor and a U.S. parent—a much more common situation."

Kirschenbaum said that at least in recent years, the IRS has been reluctant to accept, in the absence of a compelling factual showing, the position that Canada is a special market entitling the Canadian distributor to a non-routine return. The CRA often argues that the Canadian distributor is adding value—for example, through marketing expertise—that contributes to the overall profit of the enterprise beyond the contribution of a third-party comparable distributor, he said.

However, he said the United States "might be viewed as taking a Canadian perspective" in a pending U.S. Tax Court case, *GlaxoSmithKline Holdings (Americas) Inc. v. Comr.*, T.C, No. 5750-04. Kirschenbaum said the IRS in *Glaxo* "is asserting that the U.S. distributor is entitled to a non-routine return, notwithstanding intercompany arrangements that were apparently designed to limit the distributor's risks." He added that the case may have an impact on treaty negotiations between the United States and Canada.

Flexibility Versus Consistency

Despite the inconsistencies cited in the U.S. position on marketing intangibles, some practitioners said the CRA was more likely than the United States to take different positions in similar cases.

Turner said the U.S. system, with its detailed regulations, "facilitates being consistent in terms of expected results in APAs and audits. . . . The Canadian system, which is far less specific as to approach and has flexibility as to the relevant facts and circumstances, will therefore appear to be more subjective and more prone toward inconsistencies."

A common Canadian complaint is that the United States just mechanically follows its rules, and a common U.S. complaint is that Canada "makes one argument in case A and another in case B when the cases are similar," Turner said. While "there is the perception that the [Canadian] government is talking out of both sides of its mouth, Canada is saying you have to examine the individual facts and that the cases are not alike," he said. "It may be an oversimplification to say Canada emphasizes flexibility and the United States emphasizes consistency, but there is some element of truth to that."

Oatway said agreeing on a consistent approach might help the tax authorities resolve some stalled cases. "We continually deal with files on a 'one off' basis, [and] always tend to say cases are a question of facts and circumstances," he said. "This is true, but there has never been a bridging of issues."

Rules of the Road

Both Oatway and Lemelin suggested the CRA and the IRS develop a standardized process for cases involving stripped inventory from a distributor. Lemelin said countries "should sit down and define low-risk distributors, and then agree on when such a distributor deserves more than a routine return." The authorities could agree that the return should be routine unless specific tests are met—"for example, the percentage of sales that marketing intangibles represent," he said. "If you have 10 comparables, and you have an average of 10 percent of sales as marketing expenses, if the tested party has 10 percent it should get a routine return, but if it has 25 percent it should receive more than a routine return," Lemelin said.

Kirschenbaum said the countries should strive for agreement on other issues, including:

■ calculating the income to a consignment manufacturer;

■ computing asset intensity adjustments for differences in working capital under the comparable profits method or the transactional net margin method;

■ accounting for currency fluctuations; and

■ computing markups for back office activities.

Others said taxpayers as well as the IRS and the CRA should be expected to live up to standards for consistency. Wrappe said taxpayers sometimes share more information with one tax authority than the other, or shade the facts differently to the two governments. "It should mostly be about the law by the time the two governments sit down to negotiate," he said.

Site Visits

Wrappe and others also said the IRS and CRA's separate visits to a taxpayer site in an APA—or the IRS's failure to visit the site at all—could contribute to different interpretations of the taxpayer's facts. Wrappe said a joint visit would reveal whether the two governments are seeing the same facts. "If you don't find this out early, each side will base its analysis on a different interpretation of the facts and will have to redo [the analysis] once it's discovered," he said.

While the CRA usually insists on site visits as part of an APA, the IRS determines the need for such visits on a case-by-case basis. Canadian APA staff face fewer budget constraints than their counterparts at the IRS because CRA personnel travel at the applicant's expense, while the IRS charges a flat $25,000 user fee, and APA personnel share a budget with other employees in the IRS Office of Associate Chief Counsel (International) (12 *Transfer Pricing Report* 120, 6/25/03).

Kirschenbaum said a difficulty with conducting separate site visits "is that each government may have its own agenda and may not want to reveal its hand too soon." Oatway said the IRS especially seemed to "want the flexibility to delve into the facts and not show their hand to the other side."

A CRA spokeswoman said that when Canada and another tax administration agree a site visit is necessary, "the CRA prefers joint visits with the other tax administration to ensure that both sides receive the same information and facts on a file at the same time." The CRA believes this reduces the chances that facts will be interpreted differently or that one side will receive information that the other side may not be aware of, she said. "We also feel it puts less burden on the taxpayer to arrange one visit instead of two."

U.S. APA Program Director Matthew Frank said the IRS has participated in joint site visits on occasion in the past but has not found them especially useful. "We haven't found that they improve our understanding of the facts or facilitate agreement on the relevance of those facts," he said. Neither did the U.S. APA director feel that tax authorities were likely to receive different information from the taxpayer if they visited the site separately. "It has not been our experience that the taxpayer says different things to one tax authority or the other," he said.

However, Turner said that in the case of one client's APA, a joint site visit revealed that the two tax authorities were reaching different conclusions. "From the way people in the room reacted to a fact pattern, we could see that they were interpreting things differently," he said. "We were able to address the issue right then and there in real time; that helped accelerate the process and resolve what, on the surface, could have been a very prolonged case."

Joint Training

Other practitioners said joint training of U.S. and Canadian competent authority and APA staff could improve the relationship between the two countries. Several cited a March 1999 conference in Rigaud, Quebec, that they said helped bring down some of the barriers between the governments (8 *Transfer Pricing Report* 17, 5/5/99).

One part of the training—which was attended by Canadian, French, and U.S. officials—involved sample case studies. Richard Barrett, director of the IRS APA Program at the time, said the case studies were "the best thing we did." The participants were given a model APA to negotiate, and then were put on teams that included officials from each country. The teams then negotiated the APA with the help of a facilitator.

Wrappe said joint training in principled negotiations would be helpful. Moreover, he added, "I think that's the only thing that would be helpful. I believe that each government at some time has questioned the principled support for the other government's position."

Przysuski said that "from my discussions with ex-Canadian Competent Authority program members and my own experience with APAs, I am convinced that any joint formal or informal workshops or training workshops or courses would certainly help to improve the [Canada-U.S.] relationship." Apart from a discussion of the issues, he said, the joint training efforts improve the camaraderie between the officials from each country by providing a non-confrontational setting.

The March 1999 training session resulted in changes to the U.S.-Canada APA process, including the exchange of position papers as the starting point for negotiations. It was not clear, however, whether the joint training addressed one of the chief conflicts between the United States and Canada at the time: the IRS's preference for CPM and Canada's favoring transaction based methods. Following the March 1999 session, Barrett and Gary Zed, then head of Canada's Transfer Pricing and Competent Authority division, declined to comment on whether they discussed use of CPM during the training.

Scarabello said she was not hopeful that any joint training process would alleviate the problem between the United States and Canada. "The perception from U.S. companies is that Canada is out to create more money from examinations," she said. "The problem stems from a lack of willingness on the part of Canada to negotiate in good faith."

Revenue Grabbing

While practitioners said both the United States and Canada were guilty of taking positions designed to maximize the tax in their respective jurisdictions, Canada drew more criticism for its revenue-driven approach. Scarabello said the CRA "has gotten the reputation as a money grabber, with its actions being revenue driven rather than being based on good tax policy."

Ackerman said the CRA in recent years "seems more concerned with the revenue gained or lost than the technical basis of the issue—to the extent that the CRA routinely recasts unilaterally the taxpayer's business strategies." In some cases, he said, CRA officials "come up with a position that creates the largest possible adjustment."

Another U.S. practitioner said Canada has replaced the United States in the role of aggressive revenue seeking. "While the IRS may have been the primary problem in the past by being overly aggressive from a U.S. tax revenue point of view, the problem today is primarily driven by Canada's aggressive positions," he said.

The U.S. practitioner also complained that the CRA sought to exclude taxpayers entirely from APA negotiations. "This may reflect Canada's preference to deal with the other government because the government may not have as complete a grasp of the relevant facts or may not completely understand the taxpayer's methodology," he said. "In that circumstance, Canada may feel it can negotiate a more favorable agreement government-to-government without any input from the taxpayer."

Other sources said they had dealt with CRA officials who were reluctant to resolve cases in a way that would require Canada to give up more than 50 percent of the tax assessed. Because the CRA requires large corporations—even those contesting their assessments—to pay 50 percent of the assessment up front, conceding more than 50 percent would require the CRA to issue a refund check to the taxpayer, they noted.

The CRA spokeswoman said any large corporation that has filed a notice of objection or commenced a legal appeal "is still required to pay, within 90 days of the mailing of a notice of assessment, 50 percent of the amount of tax assessed." She added that the CRA may exercise discretion and accept security in lieu of the 50 percent payment in some cases.

Arbitration

Several practitioners said taxpayers should be able to seek arbitration if the relationship between the United States and Canada does not improve. While language added to the U.S.-Canada treaty in 1995 provides for voluntary arbitration, nothing in the treaty would force the negotiators to turn the case over to a panel of arbitrators. Article 14 of the relevant protocol (Protocol 3) states in part:

"Paragraph 6 provides that where the competent authorities have been unable, pursuant to the other provisions of Article XXVI, to resolve a disagreement regarding the interpretation or application of the Convention, the disagreement may, with the consent of the taxpayer and both competent authorities, be submitted for arbitration, provided the taxpayer agrees in writing to be bound by the decision of the arbitration board. *Nothing in the provision requires that any case be submitted for arbitration.* However, if a case is submitted to an arbitration board, the board's decision in that case will be binding on both Contracting States and on the taxpayer with respect to that case. [Emphasis added.]"

Oatway, who said mandatory arbitration "might become necessary" if the relationship between the United States and Canada does not improve, found the two governments equally to blame for the failure of negotiations in so many cases. Both Canada and the United States "are guilty of being more positional than they have been in the past," he said.

One reason for the aggressiveness may be that oversight bodies in both countries are putting pressure on the tax authorities to bring in revenue, Oatway said. He noted that both the CRA and the IRS are incurring greater scrutiny from such agencies, with the CRA being closely monitored by the Auditor General, the equivalent of the U.S. Government Accountability Office (formerly the General Accounting Office).

The IRS, meanwhile, has been subjected to congressional studies on the effectiveness of its transfer pricing documentation provisions and, more recently, a review of its APA Program. In launching the APA inquiry, Senate Finance Committee Chairman Charles Grassley (R-Iowa) expressed the concern that companies receiving the agreements should not be "gaming the system to evade their fair share of taxes" (11 *Transfer Pricing Report* 132, 5/29/02; 12 *Transfer Pricing Report* 711, 1/7/04).

Given that Canada and the United States over the last several years "threw a ton of money at transfer pricing, [the governments] are asking, 'What did we get for our buck?' " Oatway said. It would help matters, he added, "if they saw compliance, rather than dollars, as the goal."

JOURNALISM
THAT
MATTERS

Chapter 10

Caught in a Feedback Loop

Executives air concerns to Washington Technology, *then abandon a high-priced computer security advisory board*

When Vance Hitch, CIO at the U.S. Department of Justice, stood up at a government technology industry trade show in April 2005 to introduce a new organization addressing the challenges of federal and industry chief information security officers, or CISOs, it was hard to imagine that the group would be besieged by criticisms and would shut down just nine days later.

But driven by the coverage of the initiative in our publication, *Washington Technology*, that's exactly what happened.

The announcement by Hitch and Stephan O'Keeffe, a public relations executive whose company, O'Keefe & Company, was to provide operational support for the group, was made at FOSE, an annual trade show for federal tech executives owned by Post Newsweek Tech Media, the same company that owns our publication. FOSE is designed to give tech vendors a chance to showcase their latest products to federal IT buyers, and it gives publications like ours a chance to cover new products and initiatives as they're being launched.

The new CISO Exchange was to be the first organization for executives in the new and rapidly growing information security field, and would bring together specialists in government and the private sector to exchange best practices. And it would be high-level: Hitch and a member of Congress, Rep. Tom Davis, a prominent Northern Virginia Republican and chair of the powerful House Government Reform

WASHINGTON TECHNOLOGY

Washington Technology

www.washingtontechnology.com

Established: 1986

Publisher: PostNewsweek Tech Media

Frequency: Every other week

Characteristics: Tabloid, average 40 pages

Circulation: 40,000

Readership: Public and private technology executives, government systems integrators, IT service providers, resellers

Editorial staff: Editor-in-chief, editor, deputy editor, managing editor, assistant managing editor—online, editorial assistant, 4 staff writers

Committee, would be co-chairs.

Within hours of our initial coverage of the announcement, though, industry executives were raising concerns.

Industry sponsors on the organization's advisory board would be limited to just six companies, and the cost to get one of those spots was steep: $75,000. Executives from other companies could become corporate members at a lower cost, but attendance at the meetings would be heavily restricted: only one corporate member, selected by lottery, could attend.

The restrictions were intended to keep the group focused on operational rather than policy issues, and on action rather than talk, O'Keeffe said. And the high fee structure would help ensure only the most committed become sponsoring members.

But, as some analysts said later, the structure didn't pass the smell test. Whatever the intentions of the organizers, the structure looked questionable from the outside. It gave the appearance of exclusivity.

Two days after the announcement, Rep. Davis, saying the structure came as a surprise to him, announced he was reevaluating his commitment to the group, although he stood by the need for a regular industry exchange of best practices.

By April 12, there was more backsliding. The chairman of a prominent industry group said he was approached by members of the CISO Exchange in an attempt to restructure it in a different form, although what that restructuring might look like hadn't been worked out yet.

For each of these developments, the quick turnaround of our coverage, with immediate updates on our Web site, gave voice to critics and created a feedback loop on the issue that increasingly drove events.

By April 14, it was clear things were falling apart. Early in the day, the CIO Council, one of the main industry advisory boards and an initial backer of the Exchange, withdrew its support, followed by Davis's formal withdrawal. The CISO Exchange was officially dead.

Left in its wake were questions about how the organizers—a group of seasoned, influential executives in government and industry—could be involved in such a blunder.

We tried to answer these questions in a feature we ran in our April 18 print issue. In that article, O'Keeffe vehemently defended the CISO Exchange by comparing its structure to many other government technology initiatives in the Washington area, including, pointedly, the FOSE event owned by our parent company.

O'Keeffe's comparison of the Exchange with FOSE was a fair point and deserved a serious response, which we took pains to provide.

I was encouraged by the editors of our publication to interview several editors, our publisher, and the head of FOSE and satisfy myself that Post Newsweek Tech Media was committed to objective reporting on the CISO Exchange even though our publications share ownership with the industry show at which the Exchange was announced and at which so much technology news is created. I also interviewed academic and legal experts, getting their views on FOSE and other industry events, and how they compare to the structure of the CISO Exchange. The consensus: the CISO Exchange, in several crucial respects, created the appearance of conflict that FOSE and other trade shows avoid.

Jan Baran, senior partner in Wiley, Rein and Fielding in Washington and an expert in government ethics, said the events named by O'Keeffe—dinners, trade shows, conferences—are clearly owned and operated by private business interests, even though they may include government officials as participants. In contrast, the CISO Exchange was to be headed by two federal officials.

Federal officials may give a speech or attend a conference with private industry sponsors, but under most government ethics rules, "they cannot run an organization like this," Baran said. "It sounds like this organization was created with an expectation that the congressional and government officers would be running it. It was wrongly structured."

Most importantly, Hitch and Rep. Davis affirmed the legitimacy of the concerns by shutting down the exchange. Rep. Davis had come full

circle from being the group's founder and one of its strongest support-
ers to eventually agreeing with its critics.

—*Alice Lipowicz*

What went wrong?

*Good intentions couldn't save CISO Exchange from backlash over
$75,000 industry fees; How this public-private partnership to improve IT
security came unraveled*

By Alice Lipowicz

When Stephen O'Keeffe introduced members of the newly
formed advisory board of the Chief Information Security
Officers Exchange at an April 5 press conference, the initiative
seemed to have all the elements for success.

The exchange was to be led by Rep. Tom Davis (R-Va.), the
powerful chairman of the House Government Reform Committee,
and Vance Hitch, chief information officer of the Justice
Department and chairman of the Federal CIO Council's committee
on cybersecurity and privacy.

They were assisted by O'Keeffe, an Alexandria, Va., public relations executive who had organized and was managing the
exchange.

Although Davis did not attend the press conference, Hitch was
there and helped O'Keeffe introduce the federal CISOs who would
sit on the exchange's advisory board. Everyone agreed that an
organization bringing together industry and government experts
to improve federal cybersecurity was urgently needed.

"Our industry support has been overwhelming," O'Keeffe said
from a Washington Convention Center podium.

In less than two weeks, however, Davis and Hitch were running
away from the exchange as if it were a virus. Their main worry was
that the $75,000 fees charged to the exchange's six industry board
members might look like payments for exclusive access to the top-
level government officials on the board.

On April 14, the CISO Exchange officially shut down. To date,
the attempts to revive it in some fashion have been unsuccessful.

"This horse is dead," O'Keeffe said recently regarding the
exchange.

That the CISO Exchange collapsed so quickly is an example of how even the most experienced government and corporate executives can get tangled in a messy partnership. Davis and Hitch are among the most influential officials in federal IT policymaking, and O'Keeffe is a seasoned public relations expert with many IT clients.

But now, Hitch describes the exchange as simply a "paper proposal," Davis says he never knew about the $75,000 fees, and O'Keeffe is virtually the only one left defending it. How did they get tripped up?

'Top of the Class' IT Security

The CISO Exchange did not get much attention when Davis announced its formation in February. He unveiled the exchange as he released the Reform Committee's annual report card on federal information security, which again gave most federal agencies very low grades.

Davis has pushed for more interaction between industry and government to improve government performance, and supported the Digital Tech Corps, which lets government IT workers do stints in industry. The CISO Exchange would follow that example and "bring together federal CISOs and industry leaders to move our government to the top of the class in IT security," Davis said in a Feb. 16 press release.

Davis said the exchange would be chaired by himself and by the federal CIO Council, represented, respectively, by committee Staff Director Melissa Wojciak and Hitch. Wojciak and Hitch also would chair the exchange's advisory board, which would meet quarterly to discuss best practices and produce an annual report on federal IT security.

O'Keeffe, founder of public relations firm O'Keeffe & Company, assumed the role of executive director. O'Keeffe's firm lists among its clients government IT firms such as EzGov Inc., CDW Government Inc. and Northrop Grumman Corp., and agencies and associations, including the General Services Administration and the Armed Forces Communications and Electronics Association.

Don Upson, former technology secretary for Virginia and principal of IDG Government consulting firm in Richmond, Va., was to be a minority partner in the exchange and also was to put on programs for the group. Upson's firm lists as one of its executives Davis' wife, Jeannemarie Devolites Davis, a Republican state senator in Virginia, but there is no indication she was involved in the exchange. Mrs. Davis did not respond to several calls requesting comment.

At the FOSE 2005 trade show April 5, O'Keeffe and Hitch announced the names of the other advisory board members, including six chief information security officers from the Defense, Homeland Security, Housing and Urban Development, Justice, State and Treasury departments.

They also announced that Ken Ammon, president of government solutions for NetSec Inc., and Austin Yerks, president of business development of the federal sector for Computer Sciences Corp., would be the first two of six planned industry members on the exchange's advisory board.

"Although industry does not have the same report card, industry has the same issues," said Jane Scott Norris, State Department CISO, after the press conference.

O'Keeffe also unveiled the CISO Exchange's fee structure. The six industry sponsors who paid $75,000 would be allowed to sit on the board and to attend meetings, but the corporate exchange members who paid $25,000 or $5,000 membership fees, while receiving some benefits, would not be eligible to attend the meetings—except for a winner of a special lottery held for that purpose, he said.

'Atmospherics Don't Look Good'

Almost immediately following the press conference, questions were raised about the fees and the prospect that the fees, combined with the limited access to meetings, might create an appearance of selling exclusive access to federal officials.

"These are closed meetings where you pay your way in," Bob Woods, executive chairman of the Industry Advisory council, an IT industry group, said April 8. "The atmospherics don't look good."

Questions also arose about the legal structure of the CISO Exchange, which, chaired by two federal officials, appeared to have official federal sanction. However, it was not established as a federal advisory board under the Federal Advisory Committee Act, according to David Marin, deputy staff director for the House Government Reform Committee.

The exchange was neither a non-profit organization nor a corporation, according to O'Keeffe. Its fees were to be held in a bank account belonging to a holding company of his firm.

On April 8, Davis said he was re-evaluating his role, citing concerns over the fees and structure.

"We were not aware of fees being charged," the Reform Committee's Marin said. Davis does not want "any would-be sponsor to believe that sponsoring the exchange means they will have an inside track to him or committee staff," Marin said. Furthermore, Davis "wants to make absolutely sure that no one infers that the committee's name or resources are being used to support a commercial endeavor."

Other participants reconsidered as well. On April 11, CSC's Yerks withdrew, saying he "shared the chairman's concerns," said company spokesman Chuck Taylor.

Even so, Davis defended the exchange April 12 at Federal Sources Inc.'s annual federal outlook conference.

"This brings a cross-pollination of cultures of the private sector and the government sector," Davis said. "We stand behind it, and we think it's going to be a successful program."

Stephen O'Keeffe, executive director of the CISO Exchange, defended the organization as similar in concept to other business programs in Washington. "This is nothing new," he said.

Later the same day, however, the other co-chair, Hitch, began distancing himself from the exchange. Hitch, who had stood with O'Keeffe when the organization's advisory board was announced, now termed those announcements as premature.

"I'm not officially co-chairman yet, because [the CISO Exchange] doesn't exist yet," Hitch said. "It's a paper proposal." He added that he was examining "noncontroversial" alternatives to the exchange.

Two days later, the CISO Exchange was dead.

"We are not co-chairing," Marin said April 14. Neither Davis nor Wojciak would be involved with the group, he said.

The CIO Council also pulled out, stating it was looking to establish an exchange with industry "that is open and accessible to all members of the IT community in both the government and private sector," said Dan Matthews, vice chairman of the council.

O'Keeffe, in several calls after the collapse, seemed stunned by the turn of events and repeatedly challenged media accounts of what had occurred.

"Where is the news story?" he wrote in an e-mail to a reporter.

O'Keeffe argued that the exchange was similar to several other business programs around Washington that involve government participants, including dinners, conferences and trade shows sponsored by PostNewsweek Tech Media and *Federal Computer Week*, among others. He also said a *Washington Technology* reporter had a conflict of interest in writing about the CISO Exchange because the magazine is owned by PostNewsweek Tech Media.

The exchange had been subjected to "misinterpretation," O'Keeffe said. "This is nothing new."

Lessons Learned

In hindsight, it appears a lack of communication among its organizers contributed to the CISO Exchange's demise. But fundamental problems with the group's fees and structure ultimately brought it down.

That the six paying sponsors would meet regularly—and exclusively—with senior government officials was problematic, said Patricia Salkin, director of the Government Law Center at Albany Law School.

"It creates a public perception of advantage," Salkin said. "Whether it is undue influence or not, there is the appearance."

If an open invitation to attend had been extended to all CISO Exchange members, and if the fees had been more affordable to all, the group's fate might have been different, Salkin said.

Charging a fee, even as high as $75,000, to private sector participants to partner with a government entity might be acceptable in some major initiatives, said Lawrence Martin, director for the Center for Community Partnerships, which studies public-private partnerships, at the University of Central Florida in Orlando. But charging a $75,000 fee, limiting industry access to the six paying sponsors and closing the meetings to the public are all features likely to raise eyebrows, Martin said.

"It doesn't pass the 'smell test,'" Martin said. "I would not want to condemn it, but someone did not put a lot of thought into how

118

this would be perceived by the public."

Even so, some of the criticism might have been muted somewhat by "public education" about why the high fees and limited access were necessary to meet the goals of the group, Martin said.

O'Keeffe said the fees—totaling $450,000 from the six board members alone—would cover his own hourly management fees, staff costs for report preparation, and expenses for the meetings and an annual dinner.

But Upson, while defending the fees, agreed they were not explained well.

"It's not that the fees were bad, but there needed to be an explanation of what would be done with the money," Upson said.

Woods said simply that the $75,000 fees appeared too greedy.

"If it had been 25 grand, nobody would have paid attention," he said.

O'Keeffe cited many examples of corporate sponsors paying high fees to mingle with high-level government officials at dinners, conferences, educational forums and trade shows.

"There is a clear precedent for government executives participating in private sector, sponsor-funded initiatives," O'Keeffe said, referring to the FOSE trade show and other events owned by PostNewsweek Tech Media.

However, Jan Baran, senior partner in Wiley, Rein and Fielding in Washington and an expert in government ethics, said the events named by O'Keeffe—dinners, trade shows, conferences and such—are clearly owned and operated by private business interests, even though they may include government officials as participants. In contrast, the CISO Exchange was to be headed by two federal officials, he said.

Federal officials may give a speech or attend a conference with private industry sponsors, but under most government ethics rules, "they cannot run an organization like this," Baran said. "It sounds like this organization was created with an expectation that the congressional and government officers would be running it. It was wrongly structured."

Marin, asked about the ethics rules, said Davis believed the exchange was to be an "informal" group and became "uncomfortable," ultimately dropping out when the CISO Exchange's structure was announced.

As for the CIO Council, it "never endorsed or co-chaired the CISO Exchange," said Council Vice Chairman Matthews.

Shortly before the CISO Exchange fell apart, some of the federal officials involved approached the Industry Advisory Council to investigate the possibility of setting up a CISO partnership with that group. No formal proposal was advanced to the council, however, Woods said.

"The ball is in the CIO Council's court," he said.

But nothing looks to be happening immediately. The CIO Council is working with its own Best Practices Committee to "restructure" a forum for its CISOs, Matthews said April 29. At this time, the CIO Council is not negotiating with any private sector groups or individuals, he said.

Asked what went wrong with the exchange, Matthews said: "The CISO Exchange was structured, as originally proposed, with limited membership. That structure gave the perception of impropriety."

In the weeks following the demise of the CISO Exchange, the CIO Council began re-examining its private sector relationships.

"In the coming months, the Council will be crafting guidance to ensure that these relationships provide for close interaction between business and government while providing a clean and competitive environment for all," Karen Evans, council director and administrator of IT and e-government for the Office of Management and Budget, wrote in an e-mailed statement.

Davis also is open to ideas about forming another exchange for federal CISOs, but there is no specific proposal at this time, Marin said. While Davis "still supports the goal" of the CISO Exchange, he was uncomfortable with the group's structure and fees, Marin said.

Although O'Keeffe has dismantled the exchange, he continues to defend the group's fees and organization.

"It's a pity this program has folded," he said. "There needs to be a bright line on what is appropriate and what is not appropriate."

Reproduced with permission from Post Newsweek Tech Media.

JOURNALISM
THAT
MATTERS

Chapter 11

Switching the Current on Electrical Rebates

Manufacturers and distributors tap TED to help tame an electrical product monster

Bad business practices aren't born overnight. It can take years, even decades, to grow the kind of practices that everyone in an industry dislikes but puts up with because that's the way things are done. The problem, though, is that these bad practices can impose hidden costs, hampering innovation and productivity.

The way U.S. and Canadian electrical distributors—the companies that sell cable, wire, lighting and other electrical products—handle manufacturer rebates is just such a bad process. It got its start about 20 years ago when a handful of manufacturers, seeking to get an edge when contracts were put out to bid, came up with the idea of offering rebates under a process called special pricing authorization, or SPAs, to electrical distributors. The rebates were seen as a way to introduce price competition into the bidding process without destabilizing accepted pricing practices. But what they did was unwittingly create a system of managing pricing through rebates, requiring a distributor to file a rebate form with a manufacturer to get a refund to get the price they agreed on.

In the beginning, it wasn't too cumbersome. The process only existed with a few manufacturers. Over time, though, more manufacturers implemented different types of rebate systems (partly because they

The Electrical Distributor

www.tedmag.com

Established: 1964

Publisher: National Association of Electrical Distributors

Frequency: Monthly

Characteristics: Four-color, average 92 pages

Circulation: 27,748 (June 2005)

Readership: Electrical distributor sales people and executives in the U.S. and Canada

Editorial staff: Editor, managing editor, associate editor, associate editor/industry research, art director

learned that distributors didn't always file claims, and they ended up making more money on unclaimed refunds). Since distributors work with hundreds of manufacturers and customers, the problem escalated.

It didn't take long before the rebates became entrenched into daily business processes, but they were never particularly liked, either by the manufacturers or the distributors. They were viewed as an evil made necessary by manufacturers who were hamstrung in other ways to stand out from the crowd.

What got the industry to start down the road to recovery was a series on the issue we launched a few years ago in *The Electrical Distributor* magazine, known in the industry as *TED*.

Based on our research, we learned that distributors and manufacturers maintained full-time staff just to handle the paperwork required by SPAs. One of our columnists, Bethany Sullivan, a widely regarded industry consultant, looked into the matter further and concluded that distributors as a whole were spending an estimated $91 million per year to process rebates. In addition, manufacturers were spending something close to $40 million per year.

When you consider that the average profit margin for distributors is less than five percent, it's obvious that a cost-cutting solution would add profit to everyone's bottom line.

This first article, which ran in October 2003, produced a flurry of communication from the readership. Their letters made clear that neither distributors nor manufacturers liked the way the process had evolved.

Switching the Current on Electrical Rebates

While we knew the industry was unlikely to eliminate such an ingrained business process, it was clear that a streamlined, electronic process that was the same for every manufacturer would help both manufacturers and distributors make more profit and eliminate the hours their staff dedicated to the claiming process. To that end, we launched a series of articles under our monthly "ChannelWatch" column, with Sullivan providing much of the content, with the strategic aim of getting the industry to come together on the idea of reform.

From that beginning, an effort within the industry to reform SPA took on a life of its own, with *TED* serving as an interactive forum for the industry to participate in finding a solution. We ran articles from Sullivan and others exploring a variety of solutions, from eliminating rebates entirely to recreating the rebate process into an all-electronic system. By late 2005, we had published seven articles looking at solutions.

During the process, we also sponsored town hall-styled meetings during conferences held by our parent organization, the National Association of Electrical Distributors, in which CEOs of distribution companies and other industry leaders met with manufacturing executives to debate, at times heatedly, the issues. In the end, both sides agreed to come up with a standardized process.

To help ensure they stayed with their reform agenda, industry leaders created two task forces, one comprised of distribution employees who process rebates, and the other comprised of their counterparts on the manufacturer side. In the magazine and online, we monitored and reported on their progress.

The task forces tapped our columnist, Sullivan, to help them lay the groundwork for a new protocol by writing a recommended industry vocabulary, an inventory carrying cost calculator, and a white paper on best practices for claiming the rebate. The task forces also started working with the Industry Data Exchange Association (IDEA) Standards Committee and software vendors to automate the claiming process.

Today, an online forum is in place for people involved in the process to continue to drive acceptance of the new SPA tools, and to provide a communication tool for future tweaks of the rebate process. A "Count Me In" initiative was launched in summer 2005 as a means of furthering the process.

As of early 2006, more than 120 companies—96 distributors (representing 56% of industry sales) and 26 manufacturers (representing 80% of industry sales)—have committed to implementing the tools.

Some 200 industry professionals are typically dialing in to monthly SPA implementation Webinars.

The process continues, but the end is in sight. What took decades to evolve is rapidly being unwound, and there's a real prospect that by the end of 2006, savings from more efficient processing of rebates could start to hit companies' bottom lines.

—*Michael Martin*

ChannelWatch

Can We Cure the SPA Cancer?

By Bethany O. Sullivan

It may be impossible to do today, but if special pricing authorizations (SPAs) and rebates could be eliminated, the electrical distribution industry would be significantly better off.

Not only are SPAs and rebates the biggest aggravation in the business, both manufacturers and distributors describe them as "an evil permeating the industry." And isn't that what cancer is: a pernicious, spreading evil?

But there are treatments available. This proposed treatment plan begins with an understanding of the magnitude of the problem—and the commitment to finding a cure.

How We Were Infected

SPAs and rebates were created as tactical solutions to an industry-wide strategic problem. Channel partners approach the marketplace with conflicting goals: Manufacturers (and reps) want sales volume growth; distributors want growth in margin.

When originally conceived, SPAs and rebates were the exception rather than the rule. The intent was to support distributors in competitive situations without destabilizing prices.

However, SPAs and rebates seem to satisfy a primal urge to negotiate a better deal. There is always someone willing to take the hit on prices to gain the order, no matter how small. The result is that both manufacturers and distributors end up competing on price instead of on the value provided. It's a vicious and wasteful cycle of mistrust, razor-thin margins, exorbitant selling costs, and skyrocketing administrative fees to manage prices and recover rebates. It perpetuates the very thing it was meant to prevent (price instability), has resulted in deflation, and has left competitive openings for new channels, like home centers.

The Disease of Paperwork

The costs associated with SPAs and rebates are hard to measure because they are soft costs—they don't show up as line items on profit and loss or income statements but are costs nonetheless. They are the costs of an inefficient channel—the cost to negotiate just about every price on just about every order and the cost to administer the paperwork for SPAs and rebates. Eliminate them and the savings fall right to businesses' bottom lines.

Even harder to nail down are the opportunity costs—the monies spent attempting to make money on the buy side rather than dedicating that time and effort to creating new markets.

So how much is really being spent to administer the paperwork and back-end processing for SPAs and rebates?

One distributor with $70 million in sales has three people working full-time on the paperwork associated with SPAs and rebates. With an estimated salary and benefits of $30,000 each per year, that's an expenditure of $90,000. Extrapolated to the $70 billion industry, more than $91 million is being wasted on paper shuffling (a cost the home center channel doesn't incur).

Manufacturers are not immune to this waste either. One manufacturer related it could eliminate 40% of its finance department if SPAs and rebates were automated (as in the home center channel). That's a labor savings of approximately $240,000 per year on paper shuffling for one manufacturer alone.

As mentioned in the IDEA presentation at the NAED National Conference in May, "Driving Down Supply Chain Costs," a common language, process, and methodology for administering SPAs and rebates already exists in the form of an EDI protocol. All distributors have to do is use it.

The savings to distributors with the use of IDEA's "Pro Rebates" include a reduction of the number of "touches" from 23 to zero, the elimination in deductions with savings of $80 to $150 each, a reduction in cycle time to recover rebate money of 50 days to 60 days, and savings of up to one week in accounts receivable.

The savings to manufacturers for automating the processing of paperwork will be the result of headcount reductions in finance departments.

But the real value of automating the rebate process will be in the data provided. Once it is determined what the real net prices are, not only can more informed decisions be made, but manufacturers will also be able to set more realistic stock levels—and in the long term, craft pricing strategies that eliminate the need for SPAs and rebates altogether.

Manufacturers should require the use of EDI to claim rebates; distributors should demand the same, because eliminating the cost of administering the paperwork of SPAs and rebates will not only immediately reduce channel costs, it will also fund the cure in two other areas (which will be explored in future columns).

The industry needs to start with a clean slate, rethink the basics of its business, and develop a common vision for its future. This means focusing on core issues, not just short-term results. There's no question it's easier to be tactical than strategic, because it's hard to change cultural behaviors. But rather than perpetuating the industry's inertia on doing strategic things, let's keep our eye on the big picture

Reproduced with permission from the National Association of Electrical Distributors.

JOURNALISM
THAT
MATTERS

Chapter 12

Saying Hello to the Elephant in the Room

With help from the Journal of Government Financial Management,
policymakers take note of federal accounting reform proposals

As regularly as the cherry blossoms around the Jefferson Memorial bloom, you can count on lawmakers on Capitol Hill talking about reforming the way the U.S. government manages its business. That's when the thousands of accountants and other professionals managing the books of hundreds of federal agencies duck for cover.

It's not that federal agencies aren't in need of a management makeover; many financial management employees call the growing number of cumbersome governmental accounting rules the elephant in the room. With layers upon layers of financial management reforms heaped on accountants over the years, it's become a problem so big that no one has been able to put a name on it.

Mitch Laine, a former president of the Association of Government Accountants, deputy CFO in the U.S. Department of Education, and senior analyst at the Office of Management and Budget (OMB)—the White House bureau that keeps all the federal agencies in line—doesn't have a name for it, either. But an article he wrote with my assistance for the June 2005 issue of the *Journal of Government Financial Management* did something that was noteworthy nonetheless: he offered a solution that took just the kind of simple approach that actually gives it a chance of getting enacted. More importantly, the interest it attracted came not just from within the profession but from analysts at OMB and the U.S. Congress.

Journal of Government Financial Management

www.agacgfm.org/publications/journal/

Established: 1951

Publisher: Association of Government Accountants

Frequency: Quarterly

Characteristics: Four-color, average 72 pages

Circulation: 18,500

Readership: Public sector financial management professionals

Editorial staff: Editor, copy editor

A pair of scissors for slicing at small but key accounting irritants is at the core of its attraction. For example, rather than suggest an overhaul of the U.S. Standard General Ledger, which provides the principal reporting requirements for federal agencies, the article suggests recognizing the challenges the USSGL poses to small agencies that lack the resources to meet all of its requirements efficiently. Instead, let these agencies adapt charts of account that are simpler than what's required in the ledger, and let them submit their financial data to OMB directly in spreadsheets rather than in ledger form.

Its other recommendations are similarly specific:

■ Ease up on requirements for fine-grained loan accounting for the departments with big lending portfolios like the U.S. Department of Housing and Urban Development and the U.S. Department of Education. That one small fix would reduce staff workload significantly without affecting the quality of the reported information in a meaningful way.

■ Simplify reconciliation requirements and the presentation of information in agency financial reports, and reduce required footnotes.

■ And resist the urge to introduce internal controls in the federal government similar to what Sarbanes-Oxley—passed in the aftermath of Enron—imposes in the private sector, as some lawmakers have suggested. As a result of Sarbanes-Oxley, corporations for the first time have standards that exceed federal agencies', but that's not a reason to hike standards; to do so would not improve program efficiency and would waste staff resources.*

In short, Laine uses the piece to ask the question, "At what point

---

* OMB has since issued more stringent internal control requirements — with the shift in efforts and resources predicted in Mitch Laine's article. Agencies are investing considerable financial and human resources working with consultants and training their own financial people to achieve the new standards for compliance.

does the cost of implementing requirements for financial reporting exceed their benefits?" and then to identify the areas where overlapping and unnecessarily complex requirements could be simplified. He also challenged other financial management professionals to offer similar recommendations.

The immediate impact of the piece was to get Laine invited onto a panel at the Association of Government Accountants' national conference in the fall of 2005 to talk about reform. Afterward, David Zavada, chief of OMB's financial standards and grants branch, sought him out for his ideas. OMB also contacted John H. Hummel, partner at accounting form KPMG, who was on the panel with Laine, for his ideas.

Congress has also taken note. A few months before the piece came out, I contacted Mike Hettinger, an aide to Rep. Todd Platts (R-Pa.), a member of the House Committee on Government Reform, who was preparing to sponsor financial management reform legislation. Hettinger wanted a prepublication copy of the article to get reform ideas from a practitioner. "Congress has simply layered new laws on top of what already existed," he said. "The result is duplicative, and often obsolete reporting requirements."

This time, Hettinger said, they wanted "to reach back and reform the laws" so that "each law remains relevant to the mission of creating a more efficient and accountable government."

Laine's piece, he added, in offering "the type of specific examples we will need if this effort is to be successful," made a starting point.

For a piece that was intended to get government accountants discussing reform, what more appropriate response could we have received? Yes, the reform effort is likely to move at glacial speed, but the article may well serve as a bridge between the workforce and senior executives and policymakers, and for any reform effort to succeed, that's where it needs to start.

—Catherine A. Kreyche

Revisiting Federal Financial Management Reform

By Mitch Laine, CGFM, and Catherine A. Kreyche

The financial management reforms we have witnessed, from the CFO Act through the accelerated due dates for financial statements, set forth worthy goals. They are designed to provide greater accountability to American citizens and better information about the effectiveness of programs to improve decision-making by agencies, the U.S. Office of Management and Budget (OMB) and Congress.

Yet while we're busy implementing reforms, we need to take a step back and ask ourselves a few questions. In our zeal to reform the system, are we overburdening our work force with unnecessarily complex requirements? Assuming that is the case, how can we streamline and simplify these requirements and still provide the information necessary to support improved financial management?

We certainly need to know what programs cost and how they are performing; we need to provide good estimates to determine future costs; we need to use information to make better decisions that will enable us to allocate our resources most effectively; we need effective management controls. But we also need to be careful that we do not pursue these goals at the expense of our most critical resource, our financial management employees, who now find themselves burdened by an avalanche of requirements.

The Joint Financial Management Improvement Program's (JFMIP) September 2003 report, Building a World Class Financial Work Force: The Federal Financial Management Work Force of the Future, envisions the financial management work force serving as a strategic business partner vital to agency operations. This same report cites one of the challenges to transformation as "inefficient work processes that consume our current work force." Could, in fact, the layering of reform initiative upon reform initiative, and the attendant requirements, be contributing to the inefficiency of our work processes and blocking the transformation of our financial management work force from data processors to analysts and advisers?

Now is the time to revisit financial management requirements to see how we can continue to move forward in improving financial management while freeing up the work force for more analytical work. To get the dialogue started, in this article we target four areas: the U.S. Standard General Ledger (USSGL), loan accounting, financial reporting and internal controls. Keep in mind that other areas need to be addressed as well.

The USSGL

While the goal of USSGL implementation is worthy, compliance has created a huge burden on our accounting staffs and systems. Let's take a look at where we might exercise some judgment in using the USSGL. Within the USSGL, the 4000 series is a separate self-balancing group of accounts used for budgetary accounting, while the other accounts are used for proprietary accounting. Having "two sets of books" adds significant complexity to the design and implementation of accounting and financial systems. Many federal accountants familiar with "regular" accounting don't understand budgetary accounting and think that it is understood and used by budget staff. In many agencies, budget staff manage budget execution with spreadsheets and assume that the budgetary accounting is for the accountants and used by them. As long as agencies can properly manage budget execution and submit the required budget execution information to OMB and Treasury, do we really need to require use of the 4000 series for all agencies?

Adapting our accounting processes and financial systems to produce the 4000 data is difficult and costly, and may not be cost effective in all cases. So why not experiment?

Recognizing that elimination of the 4000 series is a heretical notion, we recommend a smaller step: Exempt a few small agencies from maintaining the 4000 series on a test basis, and track the cost savings and the results. The complexity of the USSGL is particularly a problem for small agencies, which could probably do their proprietary accounting more cost effectively using simplified accounting software and their budgetary accounting with a spreadsheet. Why not run a pilot program that would allow a few select small agencies to use a simplified chart of accounts? We could run the pilot program for two years, evaluate its impact and then determine if exemptions might benefit other agencies.

Loan Accounting

The Federal Credit Reform Act of 1990 improved accounting and budgeting by requiring disclosure of the full cost of each federal loan and federal loan guarantee program. To meet this requirement, agencies such as the U.S. Department of Housing and Urban Development (HUD) and the U.S. Department of Education must estimate all future cash flows for the loans they are extending or guaranteeing, and calculate their net present value. The issue to focus on is the OMB requirement to further subdivide each of the loan programs into "risk categories" within "cohort groups." This requires significant additional detail for each loan program's estimates, which demands complex, time-consuming accounting. The question to ask is whether this requires more detail than is warranted, particularly given that the net present value calculation is really a projection based on estimates of the future behavior of various economic factors, including interest rates. Requiring this level of detail burdens accounting staffs in the agencies that must adhere to these rules. Is the improved accuracy of the information received out of proportion to the amount of work required to produce it?

Requiring that the components of the loan costs be displayed separately on the financial statements further increases the burden. In addition, the Federal Accounting Standards Advisory Board (FASAB) now requires pages and pages of note disclosures that may only be useful to a limited number of financial statement users. Why not explore simplifying the accounting requirements by eliminating some of the risk categories? In addition, why not look to see if the number of footnote disclosures could be reduced? This might simplify the accounting and reporting burden while providing most readers of financial statements all the information they need with respect to loan programs.

Financial Reporting

Now is also the time to review the currently mandated financial statements and determine how we can convey the essential information more clearly and simply. Can we look at ways to modify financial reporting so that readers and preparers will better understand the information presented? Are there ways to make preparation of the statements less burdensome? What statements are necessary to provide information to help decision-makers? How can they be formatted so that they are understood and used?

It's hard to argue for significant changes in the format of the Statement of Net Cost. And we'll hold our comments on the Balance Sheet for another day. However, there are simple ways to improve the other four required financial statements.

The first two sections of the Statement of Budgetary Resources (SBR) display important information about budget execution. The third section addresses another important matter—net cash outlays. But currently the third section requires a reconciliation of budgetary obligations to cash outlays that actually obscures the net cash outlay information. A more direct presentation would be to show gross cash outlay less inflow, with the difference being net cash outlay. Reconciliations are an important part of good controls. But in this case, including the reconciliation in the statement presentation makes it harder for the preparer and the reader to understand the target of this section—cash flow.

The Statement of Financing is intended to reconcile the timing differences between budgetary and proprietary expenditures. The current format, however, is indecipherable to almost all readers. Worse, it is also a mystery to many preparers and auditors. We're not convinced that this statement provides valuable information to most financial statement users. But if it is going to remain a required statement, the format needs to be changed so that it starts with the budgetary number, ends with the proprietary number, and simply displays the reconciling items between the two.

The Statement of Changes in Financial Position conveys important information about the sources and uses of funds. Why not make it more useable? Why not reformat the statement so that all the sources are in one section, with all the uses in another? This is a relatively minor change that would make the statement much easier to follow and prepare.

The Statement of Custodial Activity also needs to be reformatted. Currently line items have been added to this statement that result in the last line always being zero. This statement should start with the beginning balance, display inflows and outflows, and end with the amounts being held for future distribution.

We also should be careful not to go overboard on note disclosures in the statements.

One example is the multitude of required footnotes related to loan accounting, which is addressed above. Another example is FASAB's proposal that heritage assets (stewardship land, monuments, etc.) be moved from supplementary information to the footnotes. The impact of this would be to require more detailed reporting and additional audit coverage of these assets. While this has some benefit, is this the best use of our limited staff resources, or does this prevent our staff from having the time to do more analytical work?

Internal Controls

Finally, danger lurks on the horizon in the area of internal controls. In the past, internal control requirements for the federal government have exceeded those required in the private sector. The response to Enron and other corporate scandals have brought tightened management controls to the private sector in the form of the Sarbanes-Oxley Act, which goes further than the current federal standards. There have been discussions about bringing similarly stringent control requirements to federal agencies. Why? Just because stronger controls are needed to protect and reassure the investors of publicly traded companies, does that automatically mean that they are needed, and would pass a cost-benefit test for the federal government? Or would the result of ratcheting up these requirements create a shifting of efforts and resources that won't significantly improve program management, but would likely take a further toll on an already heavily burdened financial management staff?

Conclusion

The prevailing vision within the federal government, apparently, is that federal financial management systems should do everything that is done in the private sector and a lot more. This may or may not be the best vision. In any event, visions are not realized through abstract plans—but through the efforts of human beings. And many of the human beings carrying out these reform initiatives appear to be overworked, overburdened and demoralized. In our zeal to improve financial management, we may be burdening the financial management work force with a dizzying array of detailed rules and standards that undermine the very objective the reformers are pursuing.

We need to take a fresh look at how we are moving forward to achieve our financial management goals. Others may not agree with what we have suggested for the specific areas addressed in this article, but we still think that it's time for this dialogue to begin.

It's important to ask: Will our financial management work force have the time and energy for the problem-solving and analytical and creative thinking necessary to serve as a catalyst for improving program management? Now is the time to examine the cumulative impact of the reforms instituted over the last decade and a half—and to identify where the reform efforts themselves need reforming.

JOURNALISM
THAT
MATTERS

Chapter 13

Trauma Care on Life Support

The first issue of HSToday *gets high-level attention, and prompts federal action on America's suffering trauma care system*

Do you know where the more than 7,000 people who were injured in the Sept. 11 terrorist attacks were taken for treatment? Few people do, because trauma centers command little attention. The fact is, the trauma centers in New York City—terribly under-funded like most trauma centers around the country—were so overwhelmed after the attacks that emergency responders had to send many of the injured to facilities throughout New York, New Jersey, and Connecticut. In all, gravely hurt victims had to be transported to 108 different hospitals to get the care they needed.

In the years since the attacks, the fortunes of trauma care centers have improved little. But the tide is beginning to show signs of turning, and I like to think that our coverage of the crisis in our emergency response system is helping in its own small way.

Shortly after the release in mid-2004 of the inaugural issue of *HSToday*, the homeland security magazine I edit, U.S. Rep. Curt Weldon (R-Pa.) displayed a copy of it at a House press conference and said, "There could not be a truer statement." He was referring to our story, called "The Trauma in America's Trauma Care," and pointed to the piece as he pressed the case for his legislation to beef up federal emergency care funding. "We're going to focus on this," he said. "We're going to focus on this until all American media cover this crisis."

The picture our senior correspondent Anthony Kimery painted in the *HSToday* piece is not pretty.

He learned about the extent of the crisis in our country's trauma care system by way of a seasoned hunch. He had heard that the Level 1 trauma care in his hometown, Oklahoma City, was experiencing a variety of problems. It occurred to him that these same problems were probably being experienced by other hospitals with trauma units. So, he began researching and quickly discovered his hunch was on target.

He contacted numerous authorities in the field, including the National Foundation for Trauma Care, and pieced together the seriousness of the situation and its principal underlying causes. He obtained a copy of a study, commissioned by the U.S. Department of Health and Human Services but not released for more than a year after its completion, detailing the crisis. He also researched other HHS reports and records, and U.S. General Accountability Office reports going back more than a decade, which all showed that the problems had long been known and acknowledged.

HSToday

www.hstoday.us/SetHome
Page/setHomePage.cfm

Established: 2004

Publisher: KMD Media
LLC, McLean, Va.

Frequency: Monthly

Characteristics: Four-color,
average 60 pages

Circulation: 32,000 qualified and controlled

Readership: State, local, and federal homeland security officials

Editorial staff: Editor, senior correspondent/online editor

Finally, he researched the archives of newspapers nationally, which yielded stories on local trauma centers' problems, and interviewed more than a dozen authorities and officials, on and off the record and on background.

His conclusion: state, local, and federal officials are faced with a trauma care network on life support with only the weakest prospects for resuscitating it.

Weldon's legislation had yet to pass by early 2006, but, importantly, lawmakers across the aisle were in agreement that something must be done. A growing list of congressional advocates have joined with Weldon and the National Foundation for Trauma Care to search for ways to improve the system. And new attention has been directed at the problem since the devastating hurricanes in 2005.

HSToday continues to be a key source of information about the crisis for lawmakers. In mid-2005, Kimery came out with a follow-up piece, "Emergency Response: Intensive Care Needed," which is helping to keep the spotlight focus on the issue.

But with Rep. Weldon pointing out our inaugural issue around the House, we know we're reaching an audience that's making a difference.
—*David Silverberg*

The Trauma in America's Trauma Centers

By Anthony Kimery

In the event of a terrorist attack, America's emergency healthcare network would constitute the front line — but it's facing an attack of its own; one that's quieter and more gradual, but in many ways just as deadly.

Thousands were killed Sept. 11, 2001, in New York City—that we all know. What isn't widely known is that many, many more—over 7,000—were injured, some gravely. There were so many wounded that treating them stretched the resources of the region's trauma care capabilities. Because New York City was unable to care for so many injured, victims had to be transported to 108 hospitals throughout New York, New Jersey, and Connecticut.

When an ammonium nitrate bomb with a blast equivalent to two tons of TNT was detonated April 19, 1995 in front of the Alfred P. Murrah Federal Building in downtown Oklahoma City, a local trauma center proved critical. Eighty-three survivors had to be triaged to local hospitals. The most seriously injured were rushed to Oklahoma University Medical Center's (OUMC) Level I trauma center. Six died, but that number would have been much higher had the trauma center not been only a few miles away.

Oklahoma's only trauma center now faces permanent closure. At present, it's on life support. The problem: High operating losses. Without a major infusion of state funds, it will shut its doors in June. But while OUMC is hoping for a bailout from the state, the state itself is facing a budget crisis. Oklahoma's Commissioner of Health, James Crutcher, said Feb. 15 there are "serious obstacles" that must be resolved if the trauma center is to stay open. The governor wants a substantial new tax on cigarettes to fund it.

"Since all other regional trauma centers in Oklahoma have already shut down," the closure of Oklahoma's only Level 1 trauma center would "require the most seriously injured...to be taken to Texas or Kansas, and some will not survive the long transport. In the event of a major terrorist attack, many people with serious injuries who would otherwise survive will die," states the report, U.S. Trauma Center Crisis: Lost in the Scramble for Terror Resources, published Feb. 11 by the National Foundation for Trauma Care (NFTC).

Adequate national trauma care has never been more important to the United States than it is in the aftermath of 9/11. Trauma centers are crucial to saving lives in the "golden hour" after a traumatic injury. But across the country a funding crisis is jeopardizing the entire network of trauma centers that would be the first line of response in the event of a catastrophic terrorist attack.

Furthermore, there's been no integration of trauma care with national terrorism preparedness efforts according to the report, U.S. Trauma Center Economic Status, commissioned by the Department of Health and Human Services' (HHS) Health Resources and Services Administration (HRSA), the federal agency responsible for administering state grants to develop and maintain statewide trauma programs. Not only does this study highlight the deteriorating financial condition of the nation's trauma system and the imminent closures of trauma centers that will likely occur as a consequence, but it determined that "to date, federal offices addressing homeland security issues have little contact with the field of trauma care, and attempts to connect with them have been ignored...Trauma care is not even on the agenda for the nation's response to terror, much less a priority."

Dangerous Unpreparedness

Prepared by the National Foundation for Trauma Care at the behest of the HRSA's Office of Special Programs' Division of

Health Care Emergency Preparedness, the report has been embargoed from public disclosure since it was completed in Nov., 2002. The NFTC made it available to *Homeland Security Today.*

"The last thing they want is for the public to know that we're not prepared," said Connie Potter, executive director of the Foundation's Trauma Resource Network and former administrator of the State of Oregon's trauma resource planning. "Since it is obvious HRSA isn't going to release the report, we decided we would make it public."

Potter said "HRSA agrees they have no rights to the information" collected by her organization used to support the report's conclusions.

HRSA officials were unable to be reached for comment.

Saint Vincent Catholic Medical Centers' Mark Ackermann is a board director of the NFTC and is familiar with the study. "I guess it would be most appropriate to say I can only hope that [the HRSA is] carefully studying it to make sure that they get appropriate fixes in place before they even acknowledge that they even have the report and are ready to release it...It's relatively damning ..."

"At this point in time, there is very little being done that we've been able to find out on Capitol Hill to address the issue of the numbers of trauma centers diminishing... If you look at the money in the federal budget for trauma centers, it's so minute it's hardly able to even be found," said Ackermann.

"States are working hard to try to assist, but their resources are minimal. Hospitals are losing enormous amounts of money...because the health care system in our country is broken...there's not enough reimbursement for all of this, so one of the first things that goes is what some people perceive are the extras, and those are trauma centers."

Nevertheless, "we have to tie the trauma system to terrorism preparedness — trauma systems are, and must be, considered first responders," Potter argues. Yet, Potter's group said in its new report on the crisis that "no funding for [trauma care] specific to treating serious injuries resulting from terrorist attacks has been forthcoming...Although trauma is integrally involved with virtually every terrorist response, the relationship between bioterrorism resources and state trauma funding has not materialized. Of 50 states, only four report any amount of terrorism funding directly to trauma centers or systems. The amounts reported are mostly meager."

Trauma centers are the first line of injury care in the event of a catastrophic terrorist attack. They are specifically designed for the most critical of human injuries. A Level 1 trauma center is required to have up to 16 specialists, such as neurosurgeons, spinal surgeons and orthopedic surgeons, on call or on duty at all times. If it doesn't or can't, it has to close.

Thirty trauma centers have closed since 2001, and many others are considering closure or are restricting access to the seriously injured. They are located in cities where terrorists are most likely to strike. As of Feb. 9, five Level I trauma centers have permanently closed and five have temporarily shut down. Seven Level II units have been permanently closed and four are temporarily closed. The doors to three Level III centers have been permanently shut.

Meanwhile, two Level I centers and two Level II units have been downgraded to Level III, while one Level I and two Level II units are facing closure.

"We are losing critical infrastructure in the very places we need them most!" declares the NFTC Feb. report, *U.S. Trauma Center Crisis: Lost in the Scramble for Terror Resources*. Without corrective action, the current rate of closures among the nation's 600 regional trauma centers will increase, with 10 percent to 20 percent closing within three years.

Economic Squeeze

Sixty-one regional trauma centers closed between 1988 and 1991 due to economic factors. Congress' investigative arm, the General Accounting Office (GAO), had recognized the problem as far back as May 1991 when it reported to the Senate Subcommittee on Health for Families and the Uninsured that "many hospitals that make up trauma systems are struggling to keep their centers open. Nationwide, about 60 trauma centers have closed in the past five years, leaving about 370 designated to provide trauma care. Major urban areas are particularly hard hit."

Although trauma center closures during this period included some that were not an essential part of the national "trauma safety net," what was once surplus capacity in threatened regions no longer exists. Trauma system progress was slow during the '90s, but the decade proved relatively stable with only one trauma center closure. Since 2000, however, this situation has changed dramatically for the worse. To date, only eight states have provided any significant trauma center support.

In Tennessee, hospital officials complained openly in February that five of the state's six major trauma centers still haven't received any of the $8.9 million in federal money awarded last year for hospitals. The Tennessee Department of Health spent more than half of a $2.4 million grant from the HRSA in 2002 on administrative costs, the *Chattanooga Times Free Press* reported. That included a $700,000 contract to a Maryland-based consultant to develop a plan on how to spend future grants. Tennessee has already seen the closure of the Level 1 trauma unit at the University of Tennessee Bowld Hospital.

"The escalating severity of trauma center economic challenges has seriously jeopardized organized trauma care across the nation...Thirty-one states (61 percent) report underserved areas with too few trauma centers," the NFTC study found. A full one quarter of California's residents, for example, are without nearby trauma injury services.

According to the Centers for Disease Control and Prevention (CDC), "despite evidence that trauma care systems save lives, existing systems serve only one-fourth of the U.S. population. As many as 35 percent of trauma patients who die do so because optimal acute care is not available."

An HRSA report that was made public, *2002 National Assessment of State Trauma System Development, Emergency Medical Services Resources, and Disaster Readiness for Mass Casualty Events,* notes "economic support for trauma systems appears to be a major concern among all States. The threat of inadequate funding manifests itself in the consistent uneasiness regarding the recruitment and continued retention of trauma care providers."

In the meantime, a CDC-funded program, the National Study on Costs and Outcomes of Trauma Care (NSCOT), is underway to address the Centers' programmatic interest in comparing the costs and outcomes of care provided in trauma centers and non-trauma center hospitals. This investigation "represents a critical first step in determining the cost effectiveness and efficiency of an overall systems approach to trauma care," according to a study fact paper.

While HHS is apparently waiting on the findings of the efficacy of a "systems approach" to trauma care, public health experts who worry about terrorism preparedness say the nation's network for responding to and treating trauma injuries has decayed so much that it's comparable to the national trauma system of 25 years ago—and growing worse. The economics of keeping trauma centers open—rising liability insurance premiums for trauma unit physicians and the costs associated with the legal requirement to provide care to uninsured patients—is largely faulted.

Trauma centers collectively experience a $1 billion annual loss, and with increasing costs, this problem will worsen over time. Key factors in this crisis include the fact that a disproportionate—and growing—number of trauma patients lack the means to pay or aren't covered by any kind of insurance. Medicare often won't cover operations, and state Medicaid programs reimburse hospitals very slowly.

The principal reasons for trauma center closings were recognized more than a decade ago. A 1990 national survey of 66 closed trauma centers across 14 states indicated that inadequate financing and physician participation were commonplace. The findings supported the work of other investigators and demonstrated that uncompensated care, inadequate reimbursement, high operating costs, and lack of physician support all adversely affect trauma care in both urban and suburban settings.

In May 1991, the GAO reported that closures up to that time "were due to financial losses sustained from treating the uninsured and patients covered by Medicaid and other government assisted programs." The GAO noted that many centers "may be unable to remain open without some way to stem financial losses from uninsured, Medicaid, and other government-assisted program patients."

"Although hospitals expected that operating a trauma center would be expensive, most have found the financial strain to be greater than anticipated," the GAO stated, emphasizing "many have concluded that the financial losses cannot be borne. Of the 36 trauma centers GAO reviewed, 15 have closed—12 primarily because of financial losses. Most of the currently operating trauma centers reviewed lost money. Some hospital officials said they might not be able to keep their trauma centers open in the face of continuing losses."

In 1992, the GAO again reported to Congress that, for "hospital units specializing in the treatment of severe injury, the impact of providing uncompensated treatment...is believed to be especially significant."

"We're not looking for Band-Aids here. We need long-term solutions. We need long-term tort reform, and we need to cap liability. We have to solve these overall problems [if we're going to] solve the trauma center problem," Dr. Michael Daubs of the Nevada Orthopedic Society, has said publicly.

In 2004, these same "emerging economic threats are causing a growing number of trauma centers to consider cutbacks or closure," says the NFTC. "The outlook is bleak because trauma centers are faced with declining revenues as a result of managed care, exploding costs for physician support, and rising numbers of uninsured patients...the basic problem is not the lack of economic support, but inadequate institutional infrastructure. There are weak resources and mechanisms for trauma centers to collaborate on common problems, trauma data centers are in disarray, and anemic... advocacy has resulted in an unusual void of federal, state and local support for an essential public good with a very high media profile. When trauma centers experience problems, they are largely left to their own devices for survival."

Finding Solutions

"The solution is a private/public effort in which individual trauma centers can contribute and participate," according to the NFTC. "The federal role should be to fund the research and development of a national trauma system infrastructure. It should also support specific functions for which there is a direct national interest. The nation's trauma centers can then meet the needs of America's communities, and develop an integrated capability to respond to domestic terrorism."

The role of trauma care in terrorism preparedness cannot be overstated. As the embargoed HRSA report emphasizes, "virtually all terrorist events result in traumatic injuries, and trauma centers and systems need to be prepared. Trauma centers need to expand their current disaster plans to respond to any form of terrorist event. Significant attention is needed to the contribution trauma/centers can make to support hospital preparedness for all forms of terror..."

The bottom line, Ackermann says, is "more people will die [in the event of a large-scale terrorist attack] if trauma centers are not given the kind of resources they need to stay open and to prepare for major and catastrophic terrorist events."

"When a trauma center closes, it closes to all," the withheld HRSA report makes clear. "Other hospitals in the area, without the expertise and resources of a regional trauma center, must accept seriously injured patients and provide treatment. While their nursing and medical staffs struggle to do their best, they lack the necessary skills, training and resources. Some patients will die, and others will face prolonged and poor recoveries."

Some already have died. Examples were provided during debate on a medical malpractice litigation reform bill early last year. "The crisis is real, the crisis is upon us, and the crisis is severe," said Rep. Jim Greenwood, (R-Pa.). "We have the best health care system in the world, but people will, and have, already died because they could not get to a trauma center."

"It's frightening—we've almost reached the point of no return," Potter said, adding, "this is not an episodic problem; this is a pandemic problem and it's only going to be resolved at a national level." The embargoed HRSA report itself states "the track record and trends facing trauma centers are ominous...these trends are continuing and will result in a significant portion of the nation's trauma centers closing within the next three years without increased support."

Despite the HRSA's mandate to strengthen the nation's trauma care system, though, critics complain the amount of funding obligated for it is a drop in the bucket. In October, HRSA announced $1.9 million in funding to support and strengthen state trauma systems through infrastructure development, but this translated to only about $40,000 per state; "hardly what's needed," Potter said. Funding for 2004 was stalled in Congress last fall and, as a result, a number of states have put their statewide trauma planning programs on the back burner, according to Potter and a variety of other authorities.

For their part, state officials expressed concern that HRSA funding was insufficient for states to meet the requirements of the 2002 hospital terrorism preparedness program. The GAO reported Feb. 10 that funds allocated to individual hospitals ranged from

$1,000 to $80,000. "State officials expressed concern that HRSA funding was insufficient to accomplish the 2002 goals of the cooperative agreement program," and that "some reported that HRSA funds were spread thinly across many hospitals and other health care entities." Compounding the problem, the GAO determined that states' "difficulties in increasing personnel [are] a result of state and local budget deficits." State and local officials told federal auditors that budget deficits have led to hiring freezes and reductions in critical public health personnel.

Following the 2001 anthrax attacks, Congress appropriated funds to strengthen state and local bioterrorism preparedness through the CDC's Public Health Preparedness and Response for Bioterrorism Program, and HRSA's National Bioterrorism Hospital Preparedness Program. The money was distributed in 2002 to state, municipal and territorial governments. To strengthen preparedness, the two programs required participants to complete specific activities designed to build public health and health care capacities. The 2002 cooperative agreements for both programs expired on August 30, 2003 and have not been replaced.

In addition, the Homeland Security Act of 2002 directed the HHS Secretary to set goals and priorities in developing a coordinated strategy, including benchmarks and outcome measures for evaluating progress for all public health-related activities to improve state, local and hospital preparedness. The Department of Homeland Security's (DHS) Office of Emergency Preparedness (OEP), previously part of HHS, is responsible for coordinating the federal government's emergency medical response to all types of terrorist attacks and natural disasters. Among the OEP's mission is implementation of the Metropolitan Medical Response System (MMRS) program, which is supposed to provide funding to cities that upgrade and improve their own planning and preparedness to respond to mass casualty events.

But according to the *First Mayor's Report to the Nation: Tracking Federal Homeland Security Funds Sent to the 50 State Governments*, issued in September, "officials in nearly half the survey cities (48 percent) do not believe their city government or health department had an adequate opportunity to participate in their state's planning process for public health and hospital preparedness activities to be funded through" DHS's $1.37 billion Public Health Emergency

Preparedness and Hospital Preparedness Program.

The GAO found, though, that "states reported varying degrees of progress in addressing the priority issues that HRSA required them to address, such as receipt and distribution of medications and vaccines, personal protection of health care workers, quarantine capacity and communications."

Most states reported they had not identified which hospitals in the state to target for capital improvements, nor had they assessed the need for terrorism-related diagnostic and treatment protocols and mechanisms to bring clinicians up to speed on these protocols.

The GAO found that "components of a hospital response plan not reported as complete by most states included" a mechanism to ensure the movement of equipment maintained by hospitals or emergency medical services systems to the scene of a bioterrorist event; a system that allows for the delivery of essential goods and services to patients and hospitals during a terrorist attack; and a system to ensure access to medically appropriate care to children, pregnant women, the elderly and those with disabilities in the event of an attack.

At a May 23, 2003 hearing on proposed 2004 HRSA trauma system funding, the American College of Surgeons (ACS) said in a prepared statement that "over the past decade, the [HRSA's] Trauma-EMS Program has distributed almost $25 million in funds to all 50 states and five territories. But today, even with this influx of federal monies, the United States' trauma systems remain incomplete and, unfortunately, only one fourth of the U.S. population lives in an area served by a trauma care system."

The Trauma-EMS Program was part of the Trauma Care Systems Planning and Development Act of 1990, which was enacted in response to a 1986 GAO report which found severely injured individuals in a majority of both urban and rural areas of the U.S. sampled were not receiving the benefit of trauma systems, despite considerable evidence that trauma systems improve survival rates. The Act was designed to provide states with federal funds to develop and monitor trauma care systems. Congress authorized $60 million for fiscal year 1991, and "such sums as necessary" in fiscal years 1992 and 1993—but the $60 million was never actually appropriated. In fiscal year 1992, Congress appropriated only $4.9 million to implement the provisions of the act. Through fiscal year

1995, a total of $18.8 million had been appropriated. Of this $18.8 million, though, only $12.2 million was awarded, and it was divvied up between 42 states over 3 grant years.

According to the NFTC and trauma care experts, ensuring an adequate nationwide trauma response system will require additional trauma center capacity to accommodate large numbers of injuries, support for critical access trauma centers in unserved regions, planning activities to assure preparedness of all available resources and constant training of personnel.

The ACS said "the latest findings indicate that almost half the states still lack a comprehensive trauma care system. With the events of September 11, 2001 still fresh in our minds, and with our nation's renewed focus on enhancing disaster preparedness, it is critical that the federal government increase its commitment to strengthening programs governing trauma care system planning and development. Trauma systems are a crucial component of homeland security. If a terrorist attack should occur in the U.S., the presence of a coordinated trauma system to immediately respond to the injured will save countless lives."

"One of the most important elements of an effective [mass patient] response plan is the development of hospital surge capacity," explained Jerome M. Hauer, former HHS acting Assistant Secretary for Public Health Emergency Preparedness. Hauer is concerned that hospitals have not done enough to prepare to handle mass casualties.

And they're not getting much assistance from state governments, either. "No state" had developed a federally-required "plan for the hospitals in the state to respond to an epidemic involving at least 500 patients," explained Janet Heinrich, director of GAO Health Care-Public Health Issues, in testimony before the House Committee on Government Reform in early February. "No state is fully prepared to respond to a major public health threat...Furthermore, no state reported having protocols in place for augmenting personnel in response to large influxes of patients, and few states reported having plans for sharing clinical personnel among hospitals. In addition, few states reported having the capacity to rapidly establish clinics to...provide treatment to large numbers of patients."

Heinrich further told lawmakers that "regional planning

between states is lacking, and many states lack surge capacity—the capacity to evaluate, diagnose and treat the large numbers of patients that would be present during a public health emergency."

Grim Prognosis

In the Washington, DC region, hospitals are strained on any given day without having to worry about an influx of terrorism victims. Without adding beds and personnel, Capital area facilities will be rapidly overwhelmed if thousands or even hundreds suddenly need medical attention—Washington hospital officials estimate only 400 beds could be freed during a disaster.

At a homeland security summit convened by Missouri's Rep. Ike Skelton (D. Mo.) in Jan., 28-year Army veteran, Col. (Ret.) Tim Daniel, the state's homeland security director, said "this region's hospitals could not take the load" of a large scale attack.

Dr. David Ciraulo, chief trauma surgeon for Erlanger hospital in Chattanooga, Tenn., said his hospital is also unprepared to handle massive numbers of "walking wounded."

Dr. Patrick O'Brien, head of homeland security services at the University of Tennessee Medical Center in Knoxville, said most hospitals in Tennessee have done nothing to prepare themselves. "We have thousands of health-care workers who need training," he said.

And yet, "there will be other catastrophic [terrorist] events in our country," Ackermann said. "If anybody thinks there won't, they're kidding themselves... There are going to be other mass casualty events in our country, and our trauma centers must be ready—they are on the forefront; they are where people will go."

Reproduced with permission from HSToday.

JOURNALISM
THAT
MATTERS

Chapter 14

Sounding the Alarm on the
Teacher Shortage

Led by Professionally Speaking, *Ontario's classrooms echo
with the sound of learning*

In the mid-1990s, the school system in Ontario, Canada, was
retrenching. Specialty educational programs were eliminated, funding was reduced, and recruiters from California, New Zealand, and
elsewhere were having a field day enticing away Ontario's best and
brightest young teachers. Then *Professionally Speaking,* the education
magazine based in Toronto to which I'm a regular contributor, sound-
ed the first of a series of alarms in December 1998 with an investigative piece about the coming teacher shortage. The story and its follow-
up coverage drew public attention to the problem, influenced government and universities to train more teachers, and rekindled interest
among teens and their parents in teaching as a career. By June 2005, the
magazine could pronounce the shortage over.

Our initial story certainly kicked at conventional wisdom. In the
1990s, the mainstream media in Ontario were running daily pieces that
painted a grim picture of our schools. "The atmosphere at the time had
a huge impact on people thinking about teaching as a career," says
Frank McIntyre, a human resources specialist who contributes regularly to the magazine. By 1997, applications to faculties of education had
dropped from 20,000 per year to fewer than 8,000.

At this time, the Legislative Assembly of Ontario created the

Ontario College of Teachers to regulate the teaching profession. The new college launched *Professionally Speaking* as its flagship publication and the magazine jumped on the teacher shortage immediately.

"I had six weeks to get out the first issue for May 1997," says Philip Carter, the magazine's editor, "and I called up David Stoffman, one of the co-authors of *Boom Bust & Echo*, the 1996 bestseller on demographics, to see if he could rattle something off. 'Can you do this? I pay a dollar a word. We'll call it 'Boom Bust & Teachers.' He said sure."

The piece set the stage for what became, in December 1998, our hard-hitting, much talked-about investigative piece on the looming shortage, "Crisis Ahead as Teacher Shortage Looms."

Carter ran a striking and moody cover illustration of a classroom with an empty teacher's desk. Inside, drawing on a teacher registry that gave the piece's author, Frank McIntyre, the data he needed to predict supply and demand of certified teachers, the story showed that about one quarter of Ontario's teachers planned to retire within five years, and almost half within ten. Every subject area and every part of the province would be affected. The picture for principals was even bleaker: 44 percent planned to leave within five years and 64 percent within ten.

The exodus would affect most families with school age children in Ontario. Schools would be filled with overwhelmed teachers facing bloated class sizes, vacant principals' and vice-principals' offices, quick-fix teacher training programs, and in some cases non-teachers at the front of the classroom.

"We deliberately tried to change public perception and the education community," says McIntyre. "We wanted parents and students to realize that teaching is a viable career and pump up those applications to faculties of education."

To promote the story, Carter and his colleagues in the communications department at the new teachers college organized a news conference at the Ontario Legislature. The conference attracted wide radio, television, and print coverage and gave the magazine piece huge visibility. Newsletters of education groups ran with the story, and academic journals cited it.

The provincial government, however, was not convinced. "Their immediate response was to down play our data," says McIntyre. "It was a struggle."

professionally speaking

Professionally Speaking

www.oct.ca/publications/pro fessionally_speaking

Established: May 1997

Publisher: Ontario College of Teachers

Frequency: Quarterly

Characteristics: Four-color, average 72 pages

Circulation: 189,000 (English), 12,000 (French), controlled

Readership: Certified Ontario teachers

Editorial staff: Editor, managing editor, 2 associate editors, editorial assistant, 2 review editors, 35 contributors. Design and production outsourced

Real Results

Ultimately, the article's forecasts were vindicated and, over time, galvanized the public and lawmakers to produce change. Applications to faculties of education shot up by 40 percent in September 1999, faculties of education in Ontario increased their spaces that year, the government agreed to provide funding for additional spaces, and a panel, called the Working Group on Teacher Supply and Demand, was set up to advise the Ministry of Education on the teacher shortages. In addition, two new faculties of education were opened at Ontario universities.

"The story had resonance because reporters from local papers were calling their local school boards, and officials were moaning about how they couldn't find this or that kind of teacher," says Carter.

In all, *Professionally Speaking* ran almost 20 stories over the next six years, each attacking the issue from a different angle: the chasm between openings for principals and qualified candidates, the "vanishing male teacher," the temptation to lower standards for new teachers, and the desperate need for technical studies teachers, among others.

By June 2005, the magazine could declare that only pockets of scarcity persisted. For the first time since the mid-1990s, Ontario entered a time of reduced general demand for new teachers.

"We put numbers on the problem and made it an issue for the public," says Carter.

—Beatrice Schriever

Crisis Ahead as Teacher Shortage Looms

For the first time ever, data in the College registry allows researchers to predict not only how many teachers will retire soon, but what they are qualified to teach and where in the province they live. And the data shows that shortages will hit almost every subject area and every part of the province very soon.

By Frank McIntyre

A study by the Ontario College of Teachers shows that the profession must prepare for a massive turnover in the province's teaching population. The College's databank shows that an astonishing 41,000 teachers will retire in just five years and more than 78,000 of the College's 171,500 members will reach retirement age over the next 10 years.

Ontario's school boards are already scrambling as teacher shortages begin to emerge in specialized areas – French as a Second Language, Maths, Sciences, secondary technology subjects and teachers able to provide leadership in the uses of computers in our schools. These current staffing pressures are just the leading edge of much deeper and more widespread shortages that could emerge as the fast-growing wave of teacher retirements engulfs boards across the province over the next decade.

The College's regulatory role includes alerting the profession to teacher shortages that may emerge across the province. Unexpected shortages and inadequate planning could severely limit the capacity of boards and independent schools to recruit appropriately-qualified teachers for Ontario's classrooms. Such shortages could impinge on programs and ultimately affect quality of education.

Study a First

For the first time ever in the history of forecasting teacher supply and demand, the College registry allows us to look at the entire supply of Ontario certified teachers. Whether actively working or not, living in Ontario or elsewhere, employed as a teacher or otherwise, in publicly-funded or independent schools, teaching full-time, part-time or supply, everyone certified to teach in Ontario is recorded in the College registry.

The College has examined the age distribution of the 171,500 teachers in good standing with the College as of September 1998, with particular attention to the 164,500 teachers who have Certificates of Qualification and live in Ontario.

The unique age structure and sharply rising rate of retirement among Ontario teachers is well documented. The new 85-factor retirement incentive available until the close of 2002 is further accelerating the retirement rate among Ontario teachers. The Ontario Teachers' Pension Plan Board reports that more than 10,000 teachers had decided to retire by October this year.

A return to 90-factor retirements in 2003 would slow the retirement rate for a time for those who miss this special retirement window. But even if this does happen, incentives to retire at 55 or shortly thereafter under the regular provisions of the pension plan will remain compelling for many teachers. High rates of retirement will continue until the teachers of the hiring boom in the 1960s have retired and the much smaller cohorts of teachers hired in the 1970s reach retirement age toward the end of the first decade of the 21st century.

Massive Turnover

In this College study, we project Ontario teacher retirements at five-year (2003) and 10-year (2008) intervals. Certification categories, teaching subjects and region of Ontario residence are all examined to draw out possible staffing implications across the province. The study demonstrates clearly that the profession must prepare today for a massive turnover in the Ontario teacher population.

Our analysis does not consider employment status. The population studied is all teachers with Ontario certification, a group that is much larger than those employed as full-time teachers in publicly-funded school boards. Nevertheless, given the share of the registered teachers who are currently employed as teachers, boards should anticipate retirement attrition at both elementary and secondary levels of about one in four teachers over five years and one in two by 10 years from now.

Whole Province Affected

All regions of the province are affected by the impending supply problem. We looked at the home addresses of College-registered teachers and examined the age distribution of teachers in six broad regions of the province – Central, Eastern, Southwestern, Northern and Northwestern Ontario, as well as Toronto. Although there is some variation, the pattern of one in four retirements in five years and one in two in 10 years holds for every region of the province. For the north, south, east and west, an operating assumption must be that one-half of all qualified teachers will retire by 2008.

French Problem Area

The shortage of qualified French teachers has long been a problem for Ontario school boards. Boards that are under pressure to meet parent demand for French programs should not take any comfort from the fact that teachers with French as a First Language basic certification are somewhat younger than the teacher population as a whole.

The five-year retirement projection for this group is approaching one in five and the ten-year projection shows a little more than one in three French First Language teachers retiring.

More than 1,800 French First Language certified teachers are to retire by 2003 and 3,700 by 2008. For Eastern and Northern Ontario, where the greatest number of French-language teachers reside, the 10-year retirement rate is closer to 40 per cent, with 2,900 teachers retiring over the decade in these regions.

French First Language certified teachers are also a source for French as a Second Language teachers in English-language district school boards. Demand for these teachers from both language systems is already outstripping supply. As well, some teachers with French First Language certification take up English language positions.

There are fewer than 450 French First Language candidates enrolled in 1998 in Ontario's faculties of education. Without a change in demand, or a quick turnaround in enrollments, the short supply already felt by many boards will quickly become a major staffing problem for English and French-language boards alike.

Secondary Tech Teachers

The age distribution of secondary level Technology teachers reveals an earlier than normal retirement peak. More than 1,500 –

one in three – secondary Technology teachers are expected to retire in just five years. Nearly 2,500, or 52 per cent, retire in 10 years.

Core Subjects Also Suffer

Most core secondary school teaching subjects are heading for the same extraordinary 10-year turnover. History, Mathematics, Geography, Science, and English are all heading into a decade that will see about four in 10 Junior-Intermediate or Intermediate-Senior teachers with these qualifications retire.

The decade will bring the retirement of 6,300 secondary English teachers, 5,200 teachers of History, and a huge turnover in many other core subjects: Science–4,500, Physical and Health Education–4,100, Mathematics–3,600, Geography–2,900 and French–2,600.

For the time being, the greater numbers of general subjects teachers provides staffing flexibility that eases secondary principals' ability to adjust to retirements. Nevertheless, the retirement rates are so high in History, English and Geography that the teaching profession should encourage high school and university students with these subject interests to look at teaching as a great career opportunity.

Ontario teacher education was not well-prepared for the teacher hiring blitz required for the school enrollment explosion in the 1960s. As we approach the dawn of the new century, there is little excuse to be caught off guard in planning assumptions.

The 85-factor early retirement program is assisting the profession with adjustment to the profound policy changes that are under way, especially in our high schools. At the same time, the accelerating retirement rate adds to boards' future recruitment challenges.

Past teacher surpluses and some of the changes under way in Ontario education have brought interest in teaching careers to an artificially low level. Teacher education applicants to Ontario faculties of education grew slightly in 1998 from a recent historic low in 1997. As teacher-hiring news replaces teacher-layoff news over the next few years, interest in the profession may rebound.

Emerging Principal Shortage

Retirements of teachers with principal qualifications are growing at a faster rate than the general teacher population. As would be expected, principal qualifications and principalships are often achieved when one is well into a teaching career. Our study reveals that 44 per cent of teachers with principal's qualifications are likely to retire within five years and fully 64 per cent within a decade.

Reproduced with permission from Professionally Speaking, *Ontario College of Teachers.*

JOURNALISM
THAT
MATTERS

Chapter 15

Taking the Specter Out of 'Spec Abuse'

A standards board is receptive to a truth-in-advertising plea after
PC World *gives manufacturers a reality check*

Dr. Raymond Soneira, a physicist and founder of DisplayMate Technologies, a video diagnostics company, had been doing a lot of thinking and writing a couple of years ago about what he saw as a major problem with how electronics manufacturers position their products.

Companies were committing what Soneira and others saw as "spec abuse" in which companies exploit the wiggle room in industry standards to manipulate testing processes and puff up claims about how their products perform.

Soneira took issue with the fact that each manufacturer was using its own procedures for testing LCD computer monitor contrast ratios, while claiming adherence to an industry standard. The practice made their advertising claims meaningless, he felt.

Soneira had been discussing his concerns periodically with the editors of *PC World* and other publications and in 2003 Sean Captain, a senior associate editor at the magazine, latched onto the idea and pitched it in a story meeting. "We liked it and ran with it," says Harry McCracken, the magazine's editor-in-chief. "We realized pretty quickly it was a really good story, one that really served our readers."

The story idea fit with *PC World's* tradition of examining vendor claims about product specifications, McCracken believed. Because the technology sector has a history of inconsistent testing protocols and performance puffery, the magazine years ago had established its own testing lab, which gave it the ability to take on companies toe-to-toe. "Looking at tech specs in general is one of the core things we do," McCracken says.

In this case, the lab would give them the chance to look at the monitor claims. "We felt we could only come to a conclusion about whether the spec meant anything by actually testing the monitors ourselves," McCracken says. And they would look to Soneira to help them design their analysis.

He helped the editors develop a testing protocol that, McCracken says, simulated the experience of ordinary users without jazzing up monitor settings to produce desired results, as Soneira believed some manufacturers had done. He also helped them interpret the testing data afterwards.

The process, requiring the lab to borrow some equipment and devote a substantial amount of time to the testing and writing of reports, represented a big investment for the magazine. "These [kinds of] stories involve a lot of planning and coordination," McCracken says. "You always need to allow a lot of time for them because they will always take more effort than you thought they would."

At the same time, the editors faced the risk that the results wouldn't be worth reporting. And if the opposite happened, with the results revealing significant spec abuse, "we knew that we would stir up some controversy and we didn't know exactly how the industry would respond," McCracken says. "Over the years, people have pulled advertising based on what we reported."

Even so, McCracken says, he had no intention of blinking. "If we had it all to do over again, we would do the stories exactly the same way."

As it happened, the lab found substantial discrepancies between its testing results and the figures the manufacturers publicized to tout their products. Some fared better under *PC World's* testing regimen than they had under their own, but the point remained that published contrast ratio specs were worthless as a buying guide.

Soneira was instrumental in the appearance of a similar article in *PC Magazine* around the same time and authored a third article on contrast ratios in LCD big-screen projectors in *Presentations* magazine.

With these three articles in tow, Soneira went to Edward Kelley, a scientist at the U.S. National Institute of Standards and Technology (NIST), who serves as editor for the flat panel display committee of the

PC World

www.pcworld.com

Established: 1983

Publisher: PC World Communications Inc., International Data Group

Frequency: Monthly

Characteristics: Four-color magazine, average 200 pages

Circulation: Approximately 850,000 paid subscribers

Readership: Managers who buy, use, and integrate technology products for both work and home

Editorial staff: Editor-in-chief, creative director, online editor, managing editor, 3 executive editors, assistant managing editor, 7 senior editors, 6 senior associate editors, senior reporter, 4 associate editors, senior producer, staff editor, 4 senior copy editors, Web producer, editorial production associate, editorial assistant

Video Electronics Standards Association (VESA). On the strength of the pieces, Kelley and Soneira embarked on a campaign to prompt VESA to remove ambiguities from its contrast ratio testing setup procedures. Separately, *PC World* talked to VESA and also to manufacturers about the need for greater precision.

Kelley gives Soneira credit for getting the ball rolling. "Ray woke me up to the fact that some manufacturers were violating the spirit of the VESA standard and tweaking their tests" to get unrealistic results, Kelley says. "Basically they were cheating and using the wiggle room in the VESA standard to test with monitor settings you wouldn't find in normal usage."

Kelley drafted proposed revisions that were circulated among committee members. Unfortunately, Kelley says, the committee had a full plate at the time and the matter "fell through the cracks" when he agreed to take on another VESA project. As of early 2006, the VESA flat panel display standard has not been changed, but Kelley intends to reintroduce the matter. Meanwhile, he has made his proposals available to manufacturers in a conference paper.

The story made an impression on *PC World's* readers, who rated it as one of the most valuable. Links to the article, which won an ASBPE regional Gold award, appeared on various industry-related Web sites, McCracken says.

Equally important, the effort built the editorial staff's competency in this type of reporting, which the magazine has since applied to other articles. "This story was a good framework for other stories of this type and we just very recently did one on video cables, looking at whether a really expensive video cable gives you a better TV picture than a cheap one," McCracken says. The video story followed the now-familiar template: the magazine brought in products and tested them in a lab environment to determine whether advertised specifications are a reliable guide to purchase decisions.

—Christopher M. Wright

LCD Specs: Useless?

Tested contrast ratios rarely conform to vendor' specs.

By Tom Mainelli

If you are shopping for an LCD monitor, high contrast ratio is a selling point vendors love to pitch. But if you rely on this specification, you'll have about as much luck picking a winner as you would if you bet on a racehorse because you liked its name.

Contrast ratio is the ratio of a screen's whitest white to its blackest black. A higher number generally means a better image and easier-to-read text. But PC World Test Center evaluations of 15 LCD units showed that in some cases, actual contrast ratios were below the vendors' specifications—by as much as 50 percent.

Most companies actually erred in the opposite direction, with a published contrast ratio that fell below our measured result—something that most people probably would not mind. But since shoppers have no way to tell if the manufacturer has overstated or understated contrast ratio, the specification is essentially useless for comparison purposes.

Specsmanship

We found that a major reason for this problem is vague wording in the commonly used VESA (Video Electronics Standards Association) Flat Panel Display Measurement (FPDM) standard that gives vendors considerable latitude in adjusting monitor settings when measuring contrast ratio. But this situation may be addressed soon: At least partly because of *PC World's* findings, the VESA FPDM committee is already revising the standard to provide more-detailed testing instructions.

Still, testing variations alone can't account for the most dramatic differences between our measurements and the published contrast ratios. Some companies don't even use the VESA spec. Others don't do their own testing.

The PC industry is built on specs, and LCDs aren't the first products to have the usefulness of their numbers called into question. With competition in the LCD market fierce, even a small advantage on paper can mean the difference between making or losing a big sale.

"Some markets buy on specs," explains Todd Fender, senior product manager at NEC-Mitsubishi. "The government, for example: It would buy one monitor over another if its contrast ratio was 600:1 instead of 599:1."

So important are these figures to a company's bottom line that when NEC-Mitsubishi engineers began to suspect other manufacturers were inflating specs, they tested the competition. NEC-Mitsubishi subsequently filed a lawsuit alleging that rival ViewSonic had damaged it by misstating contrast ratios for certain ViewSonic monitors.

The companies recently settled out of court, and both declined to comment on the case. But to get an idea of how widespread the problem of inaccurate specs was, the *PC World* Test Center ran a group of LCD monitors we'd recently evaluated for our Top 100 charts through a test based upon the VESA standard's instructions.

Wild Results

We developed our tests in collaboration with physicist Raymond Soneira, president of the video diagnostics company and a well-known expert in monitor testing, whose DisplayMate utility we use in our Top 100 monitor tests.

We went to considerable lengths to ensure a level playing field by subjecting all test units to a precise set of adjustments designed to standardize the LCDs. To ensure accurate measurements, we borrowed a research-class Pritchard PR-880 photometer from Chatsworth, California-based Photo Research, which develops high-precision electro-optical equipment.

Our findings? Thirteen test units posted numbers significantly different (by 10 percent or more) from their specifications, and only two LCDs—one from ViewSonic, the other from Eizo

Nanao—landed within 5 percent of the stated number, close enough to be considered accurate. The good news: Nine offered a meaningfully better contrast ratio than listed. The bad news: Four were markedly worse.

Of the vendors for which we found results significantly below their reported contrast ratios, CTX was the worst offender with its S730, which achieved a contrast ratio of 252:1, 50 percent below its stated 500:1 specification. On the other hand, our test LCD from Dell notched an impressive 892:1 contrast ratio, a whopping 78 percent higher than its stated 500:1 rating.

Note that neither our measured contrast ratio nor the percentage by which a contrast ratio missed its published specification correlated with the display's overall quality as reflected by its *PC World* star rating—which is based not only on the LCD's image quality but also on features, controls, warranty, and other factors that are important to a buying decision.

For example, LG's monitor earned four stars even though our tests showed its 405:1 contrast ratio was 10 percent less than the published 450:1. Dell's 1702FP, with its 892:1 contrast ratio, still managed only three and a half stars.

Why did so many published contrast ratios differ from our measurements? Even if you believe the vendors overstate their results to try to make their products look better than they are, that wouldn't explain why so many models tested higher than their spec.

Specs Inspected

One reason is that some vendors don't use the VESA test to measure contrast ratio. The standard is voluntary, and the spec's primary author—Edward F. Kelley, a physicist at the National Institute of Standards and Technology's Flat Panel Display Laboratory—says it's not clear how many vendors have adopted it. (Manufacturers don't have to say which standard they use, a situation VESA is seeking to correct for its own standard.)

For example, engineers at CTX haven't been using the VESA standard (though CTX spokesman Daniel Rhodes says the company is joining VESA and will be using its flat panel standard).

Even when vendors do follow the standard, results may vary due to some ambiguity in its wording, which says that testers should adjust an LCD for its intended use "and not optimize [the display] for each measurement separately."

Accordingly, most vendors adjust LCDs for real-world usage before testing. But DisplayMate's Soneira says that others use the wording as a loophole to achieve higher brightness and contrast ratios. "Some manufacturers turn up all of the controls to their maximums and then take their measurements. An LCD is actually unusable that way," Soneira says.

The VESA standard's principal author agrees. "The philosophy of the VESA FPDM was to set up the display as best possible for the intended task, for example in an office," Kelley says. "We never intended to allow anyone to misadjust the display out of its useful operating range. For anyone to interpret the FPDM any differently from that is a sad, sad mistake."

As a result of *PC World's* tests, Kelley says VESA will change the standard to precisely specify how an LCD should be adjusted for testing.

While we didn't test the monitors involved in NEC-Mitsubishi's lawsuit against ViewSonic, one of the two ViewSonic LCDs we did test exceeded its published contrast ratio slightly and another fell far below it. ViewSonic executives say that they take contrast ratio measurements seriously and use the full-white, full-black VESA test. They suggest the monitor that underperformed its contrast-ratio spec may have used a substandard LCD panel that slipped through the quality-control process at ViewSonic's panel supplier.

Duane Brozek, director of public relations at ViewSonic, says his company's specs are based on "rigorous testing.... That's not to say that sometimes something won't slip through, and we'll track down what the issue is here."

ViewSonic's practice of buying LCD modules from third-party suppliers, who provide their own specs, is fairly common in the LCD monitor business. But some vendors, including Hitachi and LG Electronics, say they use their suppliers' specs for their finished monitors without testing further—a practice that Soneira and others frown on.

A finished monitor's contrast ratio can vary from that of its LCD module, Soneira explains. "The values measured depend on the electronics, the factory calibration, and the user adjustments."

NEC-Mitsubishi uses the VESA test, but its unit tested much higher than its listed spec. That's intentional, says Richard Atanus, vice president of product development for NEC-Mitsubishi.

"We state that specification as guaranteed," Atanus explains. "There is no discrepancy and no misleading of the customer."

The bottom line for LCD shoppers? You're better off not putting too much faith in the listed numbers. Help may be close at hand. When the VESA standard is updated—probably by midyear—vendors who adhere to it will be able to promote their specs as "VESA contrast" and "VESA brightness," which should make them more meaningful for comparisons.

At *PC World*, however, our monitor ratings depend heavily on "taste tests"—actual evaluations by a jury of human beings who view a variety of text and graphic images on side-by-side displays. We believe that this kind of review is more helpful than one that's based solely on specifications—even those we can measure ourselves.

If you've got your eye on an LCD monitor for which you can't find a review from a trustworthy source, don't be swayed by a sheet of technical specifications: You're better off relying on the evidence of your own eyes.

Reproduced with permission from PC World.

JOURNALISM
THAT
MATTERS

Chapter 16

Raising a Legal Bar to Improve Children's Lives

Standards inspired by ABA Child Law Practice *give child welfare agency lawyers a target to shoot for*

Lawyers by nature are a driven, hard-working group. They strive for the best result for their clients and crave success. Try telling them that they're not living up to certain standards and you're likely to meet resistance. Keep pressing them for constructive change, though, and you might be rewarded.

Changing legal practice was what we—a team of two editors, two lawyers, and a researcher—set out to do a few years ago as we pursued an article series in our *ABA Child Law Practice* publication. The monthly newsletter is published by the Center on Children and the Law, a division of the American Bar Association.

The series targeted lawyers who represent child welfare agencies in child protection cases. In these cases typically, the agency lawyer represents the position of a child welfare agency that has removed children from a home due to abuse or neglect and placed them in agency custody. The agency develops and monitors a case plan to get the children into a legally permanent situation, including reunification with the birth family, within certain legal timeframes.

The agency lawyers in these cases face many challenges that can compromise the quality of their work—high caseloads, emotionally draining confrontations, scant time to prepare for court, minimal resources and institutional support, among others. It was also clear the status quo was leading many lawyers to make unnecessary mistakes and, in many cases, to abandon their career after only a few years.

Our goal was to identify barriers to quality agency lawyer representation and suggest practice improvements. We met and then exceeded this goal when, a few years after our series began, the American Bar Association approved a new governing protocol, *Standards of Practice for Attorneys Representing Child Welfare Agencies*, that drew heavily from our article series and now serves as a model for agency lawyers nationwide.

How We Did It

Mark Hardin, a national child welfare expert and staff lawyer at the ABA, approached our editorial staff with the idea for the series.

In his travels to courts across the country, he had observed that, despite the key role of lawyers in representing the agencies that protect foster children, many were showing up in court unprepared. They were providing little guidance to agency caseworkers.

What's more, "many agency managers and lawyers had gotten used to and had learned to accept poor practice," he says. What was worse, perhaps because of growing pessimism that the situation could ever change, "both agency managers and lawyers often resisted change that made personal demands on them."

Part of the problem of poor representation came from the top. "Many managers were reluctant to push for better representation" by lawyers, says Hardin. They were fatalistic "about the possibilities of improving representation or due to their reluctance to confront attorneys."

The pessimistic attitude of managers combined with the challenges facing attorneys—the high caseloads, an unwillingness to add yet more work to their schedule, and a preference not to rock the boat—led to an inevitable result: "agency attorneys reluctant to provide full representation or to push for improvement," says Hardin.

Establishing Credibility

Given the seriousness of our undertaking, it was clear we had to approach the topic with as much credibility as possible. We couldn't come across as crusading journalists.

At the time, we were fortunate to have a former agency lawyer coming on board the Center on Children and the Law, Mimi Laver, who joined the staff from Philadelphia, where she had represented the city Department of Human Services. In that position she had wrestled with high caseloads; clashed with agency caseworkers; stood in court with only a moment to prepare; and worked her way up into management, where she saw inadequate supervision and hiring and retention practices. In short, she understood the plight of agency lawyers and the need for changes in practice, but she was also realistic about the challenge of inspiring agency lawyers to institute reform.

To move our series forward, we created a rigorous editorial process that involved five elements: brainstorming; developing outlines and sending them through team review; drafting articles and sending them through team review; writing second article drafts and sending them through review; and then finalizing articles. Once we had concluded the series, we would compile all the pieces along with supplementary information into a book and use that to increase awareness among lawyers of the need for standards.

Through brainstorming, we identified eight article topics. Some topics were driven by legal developments. For example, a major federal law, passed in 1997, reshaped child welfare legal practice and had implications for agency lawyers. The series provided an opportunity to explain the new law's requirements to agency lawyers and how they could implement them.

Other topics grew from Hardin and Laver's experiences in the field: what agency lawyer standards could look like; guidelines for hiring agency lawyers; tips for retaining agency lawyers; using performance evaluations to strengthen agency lawyer performance; using resources well; managing caseloads; and improving agency lawyer-caseworker relations. These topics would be the keystones to improving the performance of agency lawyers.

Through group meetings, we took each topic and carried it through from idea to final article.

Brainstorming involved discussing what the article should cover, what to avoid, who to talk to, questions to answer, possible site visits, ideas for sidebars and visuals, and anything that would help give the author focus. Brainstorming got the ball rolling and provided the team approach we wanted to take rather than send Laver off on her own.

After brainstorming, Laver prepared an outline, reviewed by the team, and followed up with the first draft, which the team, and occasionally outside experts, reviewed. The reviews combined editorial expertise with experienced practitioners' knowledge. Laver then prepared a second draft, which I, the publication editor, reviewed. In the final stage, Laver and I worked together to finalize the article.

Avoiding the Aspirational

In writing the series, it was important to restrain a tendency to make these kinds of articles preachy. Laver worked diligently to avoid sprinkling her pieces with many "You shoulds" and "Do this," which could turn off readers who see the directives as unrealistic.

"Some of what I was writing about was aspirational," says Laver. "There were times when I thought, 'My God, if people read this, they're going to think I'm full of baloney.' There was no way we could have done some of what I was writing when I was in practice."

To temper the writing with a dose of reality, we asked ourselves questions that put us in the readers' shoes: "Would you do this in practice?" "Is it achievable?"

We tried as much as possible to acknowledge the readers' reality and not overwhelm them with too many new roles and responsibilities that might be difficult to live up to. We encouraged them to take baby steps and to try to incorporate some, not all, of the article suggestions.

Another challenge was that the concept of standards, which is what the articles were advocating, was controversial. One of the articles spelled out what practice standards for agency lawyers should look like, and many of the other articles were designed to raise the bar for agency lawyers and give them a baseline standard of practice.

"A lot of people think, 'That's a nice thought, but we can't do that here,'" says Laver.

ABA Child Law Practice

ABA Child Law Practice

www.abanet.org/child/clp/about.html

Established: 1978

Publisher: ABA Center on Children and the Law

Frequency: Monthly

Characteristics: Newsletter, 16 pages

Circulation: 2,500

Readership: Children's lawyers, parents' lawyers, child welfare agency lawyers, juvenile dependency and family court judges, court staff, lay child advocates, social workers, medical professionals, mental health professionals, and other professionals involved in child protection

Editorial staff: Editor-in-chief, ABA staff lawyers and researchers as needed

The reasons vary. Some lawyers don't like to be held accountable. Some resist the idea of standards, don't think they get paid enough to follow them, and don't think others should dictate their responsibilities. On the other hand, we knew many lawyers who strive to do a good job would be receptive. They're happy to see what they should be doing and to have a mechanism to hold others accountable.

Field Observations

To keep the series firmly tied to reality, we tapped a federal grant by the U.S. Department of Health and Human Services that supports the ABA's National Child Welfare Resource Center on Legal and Judicial Issues. One role of the Resource Center is to provide practical information to legal professionals to enhance the legal representation of children in the child welfare system. Since the series was an approved activity under the grant, we could access the funds for Laver's travel.

Laver conducted numerous interviews and visited agency lawyer offices in several locations. She visited Santa Clara and San Diego counties in California, where she observed effective practices that she could share in the series. Among them: holding brownbag lunches and training for caseworkers, and having office hours and consultations with clients.

These were practices she struggled with while in practice in Philadelphia. Rather than just telling readers to "hold office hours," she could show how the lawyers in these California counties were doing it and let readers mold similar processes that work for them around the examples.

Presenting the Information

Lawyers like to sound like lawyers. That means legalese, long sentences, qualifications and abstractions, and visually flat content. This is good for sounding like a lawyer, but bad for engaging already resistant readers with little time. We knew the effectiveness of the writing and design would be crucial for pulling in readers, getting them to pay attention, and inspiring them to consider what we had to say.

With that in mind, we emphasized half a dozen editorial and design tactics:

Attention-grabbing leads. For the first piece, we employed a conversational tone: "Need to know how to keep a staff of agency attorneys on their feet and happy so they will stay a while? Start by putting yourself in their shoes."

Carefully thought-out heads and subheads: In the typical structure, we started with a main topic and broke it down into several components: "How to Develop Standards" (main topic), "Form a Committee" (first component), "Conduct an Assessment" (second component), "Study Caseloads" (third component).

Easy-to-scan bulleted lists. The goal was to make the material easy to reference:

- Uncover training needs
- Identify weaknesses in the management of the office
- Identify attorneys' strengths
- Determine when an attorney is not performing at an acceptable level

Short, action-oriented sentences. We didn't want to make our lawyer readers, already pressed for time, work for the content:

"Meet with the agency administration to explain court-related concerns. Together, devise a system for caseworkers to document their case files. The system should be consistent with your needs for proving a case and their needs for providing proper casework."

Visuals to help readers see key concepts. In a key example, we created a timeline for turning the recommendations into standards of practice.

Accessible language. Especially when talking about legal matters, including legislation, the tendency is to rely on jargon. To avoid that, we tried to keep the writing conversational:

"With bipartisan support, ASFA was passed by Congress and signed into law by President Clinton in late 1997. The guiding principle of ASFA is that the 'child's health and safety shall be the paramount concern.' Congress believed many children were not safe in their homes while child welfare agencies were making efforts to preserve the family. Similarly, there was a concern that children were leaving foster care and returning to their biological families without appropriate safety measures in place."

From the Series to the Standards

Our plan to compile the series into a book, which we published as *Foundations for Success: Strengthening Your Agency Attorney Office,* was key to our aim of generating as much exposure for our recommendations as possible. In the end, it gave the ABA a concrete document from which it would build its standards of practice.

We supplemented the series of articles with additional material such as interviews, case studies, and resource lists to add color and value beyond the original pieces. As it turned out, pulling the articles together into the book helped facilitate development of the standards by creating a body of work focused on various aspects of improving agency attorney practice. For us, it also generated a little revenue, although just enough to cover production and printing costs.

At the conclusion of the series, Laver and other ABA staff were invited to review states' agency attorney standards and help some states prepare their own.

A roundtable was convened by the ABA to develop national standards, with the article series serving as a springboard for discussion. ABA staff, representatives from state court improvement projects, and other national organizations came together to talk about what agency standards could look like. Roundtable participants received copies of our articles on agency attorney standards and it was used substantially as the basis to develop the standards that the ABA ultimately endorsed. "The articles were a good first step for the standards committee," says Laver.

The standards of practice were made official in late 2004, published under the title, "Standards of Practice for Lawyers Representing Child Welfare Agencies." Today, there are signs that the standards are being embraced in the field.

"It was surprising to me how willing people were to accept the idea of standards," says Laver. "Plenty of people have come up to us and said they love the idea of standards. There has also been much dissemination, which shows the information is being embraced."

According to Hardin, "the article series was a major step toward a process of reform in agency legal representation that is still incomplete."

In the end, what started as an idea to influence changes in agency lawyer practice through an article series has grown to have a much larger impact. The ABA standards will help shape and elevate the quality of agency lawyer practice for years to come.

—*Claire Sandt Chiamulera*

Where are Your Standards?

ABA Standards Take Agency Attorneys to New Levels

By Mimi Laver

If you represent the child welfare agency, chances are you and your colleagues provide high quality representation to the agency. But is there uniformity from one attorney to the next?

When I worked at the City Solicitor's Office in Philadelphia representing the Department of Human Services, my colleagues and I felt good about the representation we offered, but uniformity of practice was a challenge. Since joining the ABA Center on Children and the Law, I have been able to study the various ways that agency attorneys operate. Over the last couple of years, I was privileged to work with an expert advisory committee to draft Standards of Practice for Attorneys Representing Child Welfare Agencies. It is my hope that agency attorneys around the country will adopt these standards.

I know there are different models of representation for child welfare agencies, but these standards apply to everyone. Some offices may wish to fine tune the standards to more closely match their own practice. I hope agency attorneys will use these standards to set their goals high, increase uniformity between attorneys in one office, and improve their own practice.

The standards are organized around:
- ■ 27 basic obligations for agency attorneys,
- ■ 4 additional ethical and practice considerations, and
- ■ 11 obligations for agency attorney managers.

After the obligation is set out, actions and commentary explain the purpose and implementation steps for each.

This article discusses a few obligations that are noteworthy or interesting for *CLP* readers. They include:

* **Advise and Counsel** – The out-of-court work you do in advising the agency about individual cases, legal training, and policy is as important as your in-court representation.

* **Case Theory** – Developing a case theory at the beginning of a case can help you and the caseworker stay on track with service provision, readying the case for permanency decision making, and ensuring positive outcomes for the children and families in the case.

* **Negotiation** – Participating in negotiation and mediation on behalf of the agency can ensure that it is done right and for good reasons, rather than as a convenience for the professionals in the case. Negotiation, when done right, can save time on a case and get all parties to buy into the case plan.

* **Appeals** – There are many reasons you may not like to appeal your judges' orders, but considering appeals in appropriate cases is essential to achieving the outcomes you want for the agency and the children and families it serves.

* **Conflict Resolution** – Create a conflict resolution plan before the conflict between you and the agency staff arises and you will decrease the conflict that exists and establish a solid protocol to follow when disagreements arise.

* **Caseloads and Salaries** – As an agency attorney manager you must take care of your attorneys and do whatever you can to decrease their stress and burnout. Caseload management and obtaining competitive salaries for the agency attorneys will go a long way towards meeting this goal.

Advise and Counsel

We all know the agency deserves excellent in-court representation. Like most agency attorneys, you probably spend time and energy strengthening your trial skills. You carefully study the Rules of Evidence and perfect your direct and cross-examination skills. The representation the agency receives outside the courtroom is at least as important as inside, but it does not usually get as much of your attention. For this reason, the standards contain two obligations, the first for the agency attorney, and the second for the managers, concerning the type of counseling the attorney should provide.

For the attorney, the standard says:

Counsel the client/agency about all legal matters related to individual cases as well as policy issues and periodically monitor cases.

For the manager:

Act as advisor, counselor, and trainer for the agency.

How often do you hear caseworkers complain "the agency

attorney doesn't represent me...they don't listen to me...they don't tell the judge what I think is important..." These complaints are often a reflection of agency attorneys who do not make out-of-court time for the caseworkers. Caseworkers must have an attorney who can answer their questions about an individual case. They need to have regular access to that attorney. Caseworkers, supervisors, and other agency staff must receive training on legal issues to perform their jobs at a high and effective level. They must know what is expected of them when they walk into court, and feel as comfortable and prepared in court as possible.

It is your job as the agency attorney to ensure these things occur. If you are an agency attorney manager it is your job to set out the manner in which it should happen. Will agency attorneys have regular office hours? Will they conduct brown bag lunch training? How will agency administration access legal advice? As an agency attorney manager, consider these, and many other, questions.

The agency attorney manager should consider developing protocols on:

■ Communication, such as regular office hours at the agency and timely responses by attorneys to agency telephone calls and emails;
■ Information sharing;
■ Conflict resolution;
■ Attorney-client work product and confidentiality issues;
■ Dealing with media and high profile cases;
■ Reviewing all court orders and communicating the results with the agency; and
■ Appellate strategies.

As the agency attorney manager, you should also ensure there is a process for agency legal training. As part of the process, you could design materials, with samples, to help caseworkers prepare for court and provide testimony. Agency training could occur during formal, new-hire training, at brown bag lunches or during after-hours courses. Topics could include, for example:

■ Overviews of state and federal laws;
■ Writing appropriate court reports and case plans;
■ Testifying in court;
■ The trial and appellate court processes; and

■ The need for and steps to complete acceptable searches for absent parents.

The role agency attorneys play as advisors and counselors is crucial, yet often underrated. It is necessary for building strong, trusting relationships with the agency staff and ensuring the smooth operation of the agency.

Case Theory

If you are an agency attorney who has practiced a while, you may sometimes fall into the trap of feeling that each case is the same. It is true there are certain patterns in cases that experienced child welfare professionals can spot. Many cases involve parental substance abuse or mental health issues. Most children suffer greatly when taken from their homes. Family members, when asked, can often provide for children. And some cases are so serious that reunification is not an appropriate goal, even at the beginning of the case. However, each case involves a child and her family, each family has its own dynamic, and each family deserves to be treated as if its case is unique. The standards state:

Develop a case theory and strategy to follow at hearings and negotiations.

By following this directive, you can focus on each case and its special circumstances. You can try to project the future of the case and think through the steps that you and the caseworker will need to take to ensure the desired outcomes.

In establishing the case theory and strategy, you should think about concurrent planning, planning for reunification for the child as well as other permanency outcomes if needed. Also consider ASFA timelines and how they will impact the case. The legal steps you take at the beginning of a case lay the groundwork for strong case planning by the agency and positive outcomes for the child and family throughout the life of the case.

For example, consider your plan if you have a new case involving two children (ages three and seven) who are taken from their substance abusing mother after she left them alone. As the first part of your strategy you should advise the caseworker to search for the father of these children and all relatives that you, the mother and children can identify. By following these steps, the case-worker is taking the legal steps necessary to document a case for future hearings, but more importantly she is doing solid casework. You should also advise the caseworker to explore treatment options with the mother, and if the mother is willing, to help her enter treatment. Frontloading any and all services for the parents, and the children, is, again, best social work practice and essential for building your legal case.

Once these initial steps have been taken and the caseworker has more information about the children's special needs and conditions as well as the parents', you and the caseworker can plan for the rest of the case. You have set the groundwork for reunification, but have also begun making a case for other permanency options if needed. If relatives surfaced during the search, then your case theory might involve steps you and the caseworker should take to qualify the rel-atives as caretakers or adoptive resources. If no relative, and no father, emerged, you and the caseworker would start to think about permanency decision making if the mother did not succeed in treat-ment. The case theory could serve as a roadmap and the map might set out a few options. By thinking these options out at the begin-ning, though, you and the caseworker will be prepared to take the steps needed as the case progresses.

The case theory and strategy should have some flexibility built in so that as you receive additional facts and information, you can amend the theory and strategy.

Negotiation

Many child abuse and neglect courts around the country use either formal or informal alternative dispute resolution (ADR) methods to resolve cases. Even when there are no ADR practices in place, parties almost always enter into negotiations about a case. Negotiation and mediation often result in a detailed agreement among parties of actions that must be taken by all participants. Generally, when agreements have been thoroughly discussed and negotiated all parties feel like they had a say in the decision and are more willing to adhere to a plan. Therefore, the Standards direct:

Participate in settlement negotiations and attempt speedy resolution of the case, when appropriate

Negotiation generally resolves a case quicker than litigation. Because of the effect of continuances and delays on a child, you should participate in settlement negotiations to promptly resolve the case. Seek training in negotiation skills to become comfortable resolving cases outside a courtroom setting. Realize that some cases or issues within a case such as visitation, placement location and sometimes permanency outcomes, can be readily resolved by negotiation. Other cases, though, may not be appropriate for ADR. This could include cases involving domestic violence or other situations in which there is a clear power issue between the parties.

Despite the positive aspects of ADR, you may feel hesitant to participate. Perhaps you've seen ADR used incorrectly where parties, including the agency, feel railroaded into a settlement. For ADR to be effective and useful for the agency, you must keep the agency's position in mind while negotiating. Certain things cannot be compromised (e.g., the child's safety, the key underlying facts of the case, or the assignment of culpability in abuse cases) and all parties should be aware of them. You do not want to reach a settlement that "gives away the store," meaning the parents must still be held responsible for their actions and the agency must still live up to its obligations. Negotiations and ADR should be used to further the best interests of the child and family, not as a convenience tool for the attorneys. If you approach negotiation with this in mind, your chance for positive results will increase.

You must communicate all settlement offers to the agency, and it is the agency's decision whether to settle.

Appeals

Many agency attorneys are not trained in appellate practice and do not handle many appeals. Most agency attorneys practice in front of the same judge all the time and do not want to anger that judge. Appeals can take a lot of time. These are some of the reasons you may hesitate to consider an appeal when the agency receives an order that is contrary to the agency's position or interests. However, appealing the *right* case can have many benefits, both in the individual case and for demonstrating to the judge and other attorneys that the agency takes its responsibilities to children and families seriously. The standards state:

Consider and discuss with the agency the possibility of appeal.

The decision to appeal should be a joint one between you and agency staff. The appeal must have an appropriate legal basis. When discussing the possibility of an appeal with the agency staff, explain the positive and negative effects of the appeal, including the impact the appeal could have on the child's best interests. For instance, if a judge made a poor decision that could negatively impact the child's future and his or her chance at permanency, an appeal should be taken. But, an appeal might unnecessarily delay a case or make "bad law" for future cases in which the agency participates. You should be able to talk about all of these issues in a way that the caseworker can understand – the caseworker is not a lawyer and should not be expected to decipher "legalese." Together, you and the agency staff, sometimes with the help of managers from the law and agency offices, can decide whether to proceed with the appeal.

The agency attorney should not decide against an appeal because of concern about the trial judge's reaction, the attorney's lack of familiarity with appellate process or concern about the length of time it will take to prepare the appeal. If necessary, work with a more experienced appellate attorney on this part of the case. Once the decision to appeal has been made, other Standards direct you on how to proceed.

Conflict Resolution

Because you work so closely with agency staff on difficult and emotional issues, disagreements and misunderstandings are inevitable. For this reason, the standards instruct:

Ensure a conflict resolution system is created.

It is much better for everyone if the system is established before conflict occurs. That way, as soon as you and the caseworker disagree, or two agency staff members disagree, you can start the process to resolve the concerns. Neither person should feel angry that a formal process is being invoked; that is why it was created.

Areas that often lead to conflict include: disagreement about the way a case is being handled, concern that a petition is not getting filed (or filed soon enough), distrust of each other, lack of timely communication, lawyers and caseworkers not "speaking the same language," concern that a caseworker does not have proper documents in her file, or caseworkers feeling that attorneys have not taken the time to prepare them thoroughly for a trial.

The agency attorney/agency attorney manager and agency should jointly develop a conflict resolution system to cover attorney-caseworker conflict and conflicts among caseworkers and other agency staff.

Key principles of the system should include: 1) the attorney and caseworker (or two caseworkers) should start with a face-to-face meeting to try to resolve the conflict; 2) if there is no resolution, the system should clearly say how each person should go up their respective chains of command; and 3) the system should set out examples of issues that are legal and those that are social work decisions, understanding that most issues will need to be resolved jointly. The system should incorporate timeframes for resolution so a case is not delayed.

Once the system is created, it is important that agency staff and all the agency attorneys know the system exists and that management wants staff to use it. Staff should not receive the message that they would be punished for asking for a conflict to be resolved in this formal way.

Developing a conflict resolution system is one way to resolve conflict. As you and the agency work together to put the system in place, you will learn where the actual and potential areas of disagreement already are so you can work in a systemic way to reduce them. This process will also alert staff that management values a strong working relationship between the attorneys and staff as well as between staff members themselves.

Caseloads

Most agency attorneys are overworked and have a caseload that is difficult to manage. High caseload is one of the major barriers to quality representation and a source of high attorney stress and turnover. How attorneys define cases and attorney obligations vary

180

from place to place, but having a manageable caseload is crucial. One study found that a caseload of 40-50 active cases is reasonable, and a caseload of over 60 cases is unmanageable. The standards drafting committee recommended a caseload of no more than 60 and directed agency attorney managers to:

Determine and set reasonable caseloads for agency attorneys.

An agency attorney manager should determine reasonable caseload levels for the agency attorneys and then monitor the attorneys to ensure they do not carry more than that number. The manager could consider a caseload/workload study, review written materials about such studies, or look into caseload sizes in similar counties to accurately determine the ideal caseload for attorneys in the office.

When deciding on the appropriate number of cases, the manager should remember to account for all agency attorney obligations, case difficulty, the time required to thoroughly prepare a case, support staff assistance, travel time, level of experience of attorneys, and available time (excluding vacation, holidays, sick leave, training and other non-case-related activity). A caseload review that does not consider these issues will not account for all the things that take an attorney's time. The result will be a caseload that is still too large and leaves the attorney feeling as stressed as before the review.

If the agency attorney manager carries a caseload, the number of cases should reflect the time the individual spends on management duties.

Salaries

Like caseload, salary is an issue that leads to burnout and stress. As an agency attorney you're likely to care greatly about children and families and want to perform at a high level. However, you must also financially support yourself and feel good about your work. Low salaries result in less experienced attorneys taking the agency attorney job. With greater experience, you may be tempted to leave for a higher paying position. The standards direct agency attorney managers to:

Advocate for competitive salaries for staff attorneys.

As an agency attorney manager, you should advocate for salaries for the agency attorneys that are competitive with other government attorneys, such as District Attorneys, Public Defenders or County Attorneys/Solicitors, in your jurisdiction. You will need to learn who in your jurisdiction makes budget decisions that impact the agency attorneys, and approach them with your request. It could be your city council, court, mayor or other body, but you must appeal to their sense of fairness and concern for the children and families in your community. You may need to educate this entity about the relationship between experienced agency attorneys and positive outcomes for the agency and ultimately the children and families. Offer to provide national statistics, these practice standards and information about the importance of the agency attorney to the child welfare process, and be prepared to explain the connection between salary and these better outcomes.

Your advocacy is important for the individual agency attorneys, but it also communicates to the agency and the community that the agency attorney manager believes that child welfare professionals deserve the income and respect of their counterparts in other government offices. Unfortunately, in many jurisdictions, child welfare is still considered less important than other kinds of law. This is unacceptable.

Conclusion

These practice standards provide an opportunity for agency attorneys and their managers to take a good look at themselves to see where there is room for improvement. Most agency attorneys will already do much of what the standards suggest, but there is always room for growth. Child welfare agencies deserve the highest level of representation; otherwise children and families suffer. I hope these standards help agency attorneys understand the need for that level of representation and deliver it for their agency.

Reproduced with permission from ABA Child Law Practice.

JOURNALISM
THAT
MATTERS

Chapter 17

Better Ideas, Better Security

*A company puts its guard contractor on the hook to earn all of its pay—
just like in a* Security Management *case study*

Given the bottom-line demands of the business environment in which security professionals manage their departments, readers of our magazine, *Security Management*, are hungry for tested ideas on how they can motivate staff and service providers to meet high-performance standards without racking up huge bills. Those ideas are something we've been able to provide in our pages thanks to the readers themselves: whenever they develop security solutions in their fields, they come to us to share what they've learned with others. With this relationship as its foundation, *Security Management* has evolved into an industry forum for the sharing of best practices.

"The Path to Peak Performance," which ran in March 2004, highlights the power of the forum because it led another security official to develop a new program after he read about the author's approach in the magazine.

The author of that piece, Glenn Sandford, was manager of corporate security and safety at Gannett Company — publisher of *USA Today*, among other publications — and a holder of the industry's Certified Protection Professional designation. Sandford came to us with an article proposal about how he met a challenge that all managers, not just those in security, deal with today: When your company directs you to outsource vital services, such as security guard patrols, how do you increase your chances that the provider of those services will live up to your standards and at a price that conforms to your budget limitations?

Sandford found a way. He used an approach called performance-based management to establish a system of accountability for service providers to create benchmarks and incentives for excellence. He then provided a concise explanation of how the system worked in his article.

Under Sandford's approach, the vendor who would be providing security officers for the corporate headquarters Gannett was then building in McLean, Va., would not just get a set fee per hours worked, the typical industry practice. Instead, the company agreed that part of the payment would depend on whether guards met performance criteria. The company and Sandford then worked together to develop those criteria and how to test whether they had been met. Both Gannett and the vendor would have money at stake in the performance of the officers, so it was crucial for both to have a hand in how the test would measure performance.

From the vendor's perspective, there was a concern that Gannett would require testing so rigorous it would be difficult to pass, while Gannett had to be assured that testing would be stringent enough to eliminate the possibility of artificially inflated scores. Because a history of frank dialogue had been established, however, both Gannett and the provider were confident they were entering a partnership with the single vision of quality assurance.

To build the incentive, Gannett agreed to pay the vendor 110 percent of certain pooled funds when success was achieved in selected categories they had agreed upon: customer satisfaction, job knowledge, and customer service. The vendor supported the other incentives by agreeing to forgo some of its funds from the pool if performance requirements were not met. And to ensure that line staff profited from the fruits of their labor, a percentage of the award was made available for distribution to the officers, at the discretion of the contract account manager.

When the piece appeared in the magazine, Vance Toler, director of corporate security with Southwest Airlines Company in Dallas was struggling with the same issue—how to develop performance metrics. In his case, it would be for the contract services being used to support the corporate security investigation and building security groups within his company.

"I wanted a way to improve performance and make sure we could measure that improvement in a standardized way," Toler says. "When I came across this article, it represented a unique and logical and reasonable method of not only rewarding your employees but improving their performance while doing so."

Toler had heard of the concept of performance-based management as it applied to other fields. But was it something that could reasonably be done with a security staff? "After reading the article, I realized it could," he says.

Toler's situation is somewhat different than that at Gannett. He has a smaller security staff and a different type of campus to protect. But the article, he says, "gave me insight into how they developed the criteria and how they weighted values in terms of significance. We are now trying to apply those to our security staff and determine how we will measure it and what values will apply to each area."

He has obtained management buy-in to the concept, and if everything goes smoothly in hashing out the details with the service provider, he says, he hopes to implement the system in 2006.

Through that type of one-on-one reader education, *Security Management* helps security professionals do their jobs better—and that makes everyone they serve more secure. In the end, it also makes the industry more professional. What's more, it shows the integral role of trade publications in moving industry leaders to make concrete changes in how they do their work.

-Sherry L. Harowitz

SECURITY MANAGEMENT

Security Management

www.securitymanagement.com/

Established: 1957

Publisher: ASIS International, Alexandria, Va.

Frequency: Monthly

Characteristics: Four-color, average 120 pages

Circulation: 33,000, paid

Readership: Security executives, mid-level and top management. Most work in mid-size to large organizations that span multiple sectors, ranging from manufacturing sites to universities and museums

Editorial staff: Editor-in-chief and six writers/editors. Art and production handled by a separate three-person staff

The Path to Peak Performance

By Glenn W. Sandford, CPP

When Gannett Co., Inc., was preparing to move into a new headquarters facility in McLean, Virginia, a Washington, D.C., suburb, the company's security director set out to identify innovative solutions to protect the 1.5 million-square-foot building and 25-acre campus, which when completed would house more than 1,600 of the media giant's employees.

Gannett has a minimal in-house security staff consisting of one corporate security and safety manager (the author), who falls under the facilities function. The company relies on contract officers for its security needs, which include patrolling the building and grounds, assisting with parking, taking care of visitor access, handling special security needs for large or high-profile events, and performing a host of other services.

At the time of the move, the company hired a consulting firm, UMS Group, to reexamine its facility management outsourcing strategies. With regard to security operations, the objective was to maximize guard performance while minimizing costs and staffing levels. While still at its previous location, Gannett had decided to switch service providers at the time of the move to the new headquarters.

The Plan

Performance-based management (sometimes referred to as management by objective) was selected as the tool of choice for all of the major service contracts, not just those involving security. As a part of this process, Gannett management had to identify meaningful goals and metrics for contract staff and establish a system of rewards for service providers when those goals were met.

In Gannett's view, a performance-based contract meant that the provider had to be willing to support these efforts financially, putting some of its profit at risk if goals were not met. As a first step in creating these metrics to identify, measure, and reward success, Gannett established a working partnership based on honesty, candor, and open communications. From the beginning, the company met repeatedly with its selected provider to brainstorm approaches and to answer two essential questions: What constitutes quality service, and how can quality be defined at a level where it allows staff to be aware of expectations and motivated to meet them?

Metrics

Following this extensive dialog, six elements were chosen as quality assurance indicators: job knowledge, customer service, customer satisfaction, innovation, turnover, and building stewardship. When combined, these measures provide a representative mosaic of the overall quality and performance of the security staff, particularly in relation to performance in the eyes of security's customers, which are defined as the building's occupants, whether visitors or staff.

These quality-assurance indicators made it clear that security staff should focus primarily on customer care rather than on housekeeping issues such as timeliness and appearance. Additionally, they provided a framework in which the contract security manager could design any number of creative training and testing mechanisms to keep the work stimulating for staff.

Each of the elements was definitively measured so that a numerical rating could be assigned to the behaviors, which were separated by shift. Building stewardship, for example, was measured only by the number of work tickets turned in quarterly and carried a weight of 10 percent of the overall rating. Meanwhile, job knowledge was given a weight of 25 percent and used drill scenarios, pen-and-paper tests, and secret shoppers to rate 100 percent of supervisors and 80 percent of line staff (the vendor decided who it wanted to test and when the test would be given).

All of the metrics are evaluated quarterly to ensure that the focus remains on the overall trend rather than on daily fluctuations. One exception is customer satisfaction, which is calculated annually using an employee survey. (More on this later.)

Likewise, innovation measures the steps the vendor and staff have taken to save money, improve service, and so on. In this case, the staff person must lay out the idea—the current situation, the proposed solution, and the measurement to be used—and, if the idea is approved by Gannett, must follow the idea through to implementation to receive credit. For example, someone might suggest that by restriping certain traffic lanes, the possibility for vehicle accidents could be reduced. Thus far, the most successful innovations have related to parking and traffic control issues.

A team of four—the vendor's director for business development and local manager, the author, and a facilities analyst at Gannett—developed the first set of metrics and the reward system. Now, the vendor is responsible for designing the tests and self-assessments, though all of the test material is reviewed jointly with Gannett management prior to use, and review meetings are held.

Reward System

The metrics become motivational tools through a reward system structured around the six factors. Under this system, a percentage of the vendor's profit is put at risk, depending on the security staff's success in complying with or meeting the requirements of the six quality assurance indicators; ranges of scores correspond to some percentage of the profit at risk that the vendor will receive for that score. Each of the six metrics is worth a different percentage of the total profit at risk.

Let's say that the profit at risk is $1 for each billable hour. If 1,000 hours are worked during the quarter, this is equal to $1,000 at risk. As job knowledge scores carry a weight of 25 percent of the total metric, the job knowledge ranges will apply to $250 of the profit at risk. For our example, assume that a shift has an average score of 88. In this category, average scores between 85 and 89 percent earn 90 percent of the profit at risk, or $225.

Developing the reward mechanism required the greatest extension of trust by both parties and the greatest depth of forethought. For example, the vendor and Gannett realized that the profit at risk had to be awarded after the quarterly review meetings for it to be perceived as a reward for performance. To do otherwise might have required the vendor to return money if the desired results had not been achieved, thus creating the impression that the system was penalty based. The profit at risk also had to be sufficient to drive and reinforce the desired behaviors without being so large as to dissuade the service provider from participating altogether.

From the vendor's perspective, there was a natural concern that Gannett might require testing so rigorous as to be too difficult to pass, while on the flip side, Gannett had to be assured that vendor testing procedures would be stringent enough to eliminate the possibility of artificially inflated scores. Because a history of frank and open dialogue had already been established, however, both Gannett and the provider were confident that they were entering a partnership with the single vision of quality assurance.

Ultimately, both entities funded the incentive pool, with Gannett agreeing to pay the vendor 110 percent of the profit at risk when success was achieved in the categories of customer satisfaction, job knowledge, and customer service. The vendor supported the other incentives by agreeing to forgo some of its profit if performance requirements were not met. And to ensure that line staff profited from the fruits of their labor, a percentage of the award was made available for distribution to the officers, at the discretion of the contract account manager.

Implementation

Gannett and its service provider agreed to wait six months after security staff began operations at the new campus in April 2001 before bringing the performance metrics component on board; by that point, Gannett's employees had started to move to the site. This allowed security staff a window of opportunity to become familiar with their new surroundings, equipment, and post orders. It also provided the account manager with time to identify areas needing improvement, train staff to correct these deficiencies, and subsequently test officers and supervisors on the material.

Testing

The creation and preparation of the test material proved to be a difficult task, with the parties working together to formulate and script questions that would appropriately assess each officer's knowledge and abilities while ensuring that the goal of a passing score was reasonably achievable. In the end, practice testing during the first quarter required a last-minute push by the vendor to ensure that all criteria created jointly by the vendor and Gannett had been met—for instance, that 100 percent of supervisors and 80 percent of nonsupervisory staff be tested in job knowledge and customer service.

The fiber of the relationship was tested when the results of the first set of written tests in the job knowledge category yielded an average score of only 71 percent. Wanting to correct this situation before the scores were considered permanent, the vendor asked for an opportunity to retest the officers. This raised the philosophical question of whether the purpose of the testing was to create a snapshot view of strengths and weaknesses, which would determine the period's results, or whether it was to serve as an ongoing barometer of achievement, which would be an impetus for improvement. If the latter were the case, the vendor would be given a chance to correct the deficiencies through additional training and testing prior to the end of the quarter.

The two parties took this opportunity to review their commitments to the design of the system and identify what, if any, future advantage might be gained for both options. Without hesitation or reservations, Gannett's service provider agreed that the spirit of the agreement was more important than any immediate need to realize profit; it elected to let the scores stand and live with the results.

The approach paid off. The next round of tests yielded some very good results. For innovation, the vendor scored 100 percent; in job knowledge, 90 percent; in customer service, 96 percent; in building stewardship, 100 percent; and in turnover, 23 percent. (Customer satisfaction was not included in the first quarter metrics because it is measured annually.)

Over time, the process of generating test material became easier; at the same time, the design of the tests and the content itself grew more difficult. Since the implementation of the program, testing formats migrated from multiple choice to fill-in-the-blank and to questions requiring short narrative answers. The tests now require more effort and seek more thorough information and knowledge. In some instances, important multiple-part questions such as identifying the action steps for the complete management of a building fire alarm were graded as "all or nothing" responses.

As rank-and-file staff became more experienced and more knowledgeable about the purpose and benefits of quarterly testing, they began to submit their own questions and ideas. Soon, such efforts spawned friendly competition among the officers, as they vied to see who could submit the most difficult question or innovative idea. There has also been some competition between shifts (scores are presented by shift), particularly because some of the bonus funds are awarded by shift. (They are divided among line officers by the shift captain.)

Results

By and large, the general feedback from staff has demonstrated that once employees understand the metrics program and why it exists, they like that the program helps keep the job interesting and allows them a quarterly bonus if their performance is up to snuff. This provides an incentive for staff to improve their performance. It has also kept turnover low.

Gannett has also discovered that as security officers have longer tenures at the company, the vendor has been able to make a substantive shift in the way training is being conducted. Typical training programs in the security guard industry consist of a series of building-block lessons designed to provide an officer with increasing competency in a specific skill set or area of knowledge. Often, however, officers learn the "how" without the "why."

Security officers who can understand and articulate not just what they do but also why they do it will exercise better judgment when faced with unforeseen events and circumstances that force them to act without a script. Training for Gannett officers now focuses on the why as well as the how. This approach allows them to be better problem solvers.

For instance, consider Gannett's emergency evacuation procedures. These dictate that security officers move to designated exit points from floors into stairwells; once there, officers obtain headcounts from employee safety coordinators as to how many people are left on the floor. Then they are to report those figures to the supervisor at the security console.

If the security officer knows that two people remain on the floor and waits until after the drill is complete or the incident is investigated before reporting it to the supervisor, this would technically be correct, according to procedure. However, if they know why they are collecting such information—to relay the information to emergency responders so that they will be aware the building is not clear—officers are more likely to complete the task with dispatch.

Since those first days of the program, metrics scores have increased as the officers' knowledge base has grown. In June 2003, Gannett's security provider achieved a high score in all categories for the first time. Especially noteworthy was the 94.9 percent approval rating on the annual customer satisfaction survey.

Both parties are pleased with the results, but both also know they cannot rest on their laurels. The success of the metrics program lies in its requirement for continual improvement, and the next step in the evolution is always just over the horizon.

Through hard work, communication, and trust the metrics system has paid off big for the vendor and Gannett. The provider has earned more money than if it had a standard contract, and employee confidence in the security staff has risen to an unprecedented level. Now that's news.

JOURNALISM
THAT
MATTERS

Chapter 18

Rattling the Electricity Pricing Cage

A heretical pricing idea, floated in Public Power,
survives to fight another day

Public power executives aren't typically known for their literary
interests, but in June 2004 industry officials were hotly debating
the meaning of a fable that appeared in that month's issue of *Public
Power* magazine:

A Pricing Fable

Jane operated a nice restaurant and was always on the lookout for
ways to earn more profits. One day she decided to sell after-dinner
mints. She placed them on the counter next to the cash register so all
the customers would see them as they left the restaurant. The mints
took up little space and required Jane to incur no new significant
expenses other than for the mints. She bought the mints for 30 cents
each and sold them for 50 cents each, thereby earning a profit of 20
cents on each mint. The mints were a big hit and soon Jane was selling
1,000 per month, and earning $200 in profits.

Jane thought she had a nice moneymaker in mints. Then she talked
to her accountant, Joe. Joe pointed out that the mints take up 0.05 percent of the floor space of the restaurant and therefore should be allocated that share of the lighting expense, the mortgage on the building
and equipment, the labor benefits on Bill the cook, and all other overhead costs. After spending a few minutes with his pocket calculator, Joe

informed Jane that she must add 21 cents in overhead costs for each mint. Anything short of this would not recover the full costs of the mint and Jane would be losing money.

"You see, Jane," said Joe with a calm smile on his face, "you haven't been making $200 per month in profits on your mints, because you've left out the overhead costs. You are actually losing one cent on each mint. Therefore, you are losing $10 per month!" Jane trusted Joe. She stopped selling the mints.

As the years went by, Jane often wondered how she could have been so foolish as to think that buying mints at 30 cents and selling them for 50 cents could make her any money, so she started applying Joe's advice to additional operations of her restaurant, starting with her wine. She realized that her wine was in the same position as the mints. Up until then she had figured that if she sold each bottle for more than it cost her, she would make money. But Joe showed her how wrong this was, and the picture cleared right up when she allocated overhead costs to the wine. Eventually, Jane cut wine from her menu.

Jane eventually lost her restaurant due to bankruptcy from lack of sales. She now works the cash register on the late shift at another restaurant across town. Her new boss has told her how important it is to push the after-dinner mints prominently displayed on the counter. "You'd be surprised how much money we make off these things," her boss said on her first day on the job.

No one is sure where Joe is these days. There are rumors that he went to work for a public utility somewhere in the Northwest, but one thing is clear: he's got a good job. There's always a market for a guy who knows how to allocate overhead costs.

———————————

The fable was written by Mike McMahon, senior manager of economics and business consulting for the Snohomish County Public Utility District in Washington. His purpose was to help lift the fog from the brains of utility executives around the country. That fog had settled after John Kelly, director of economics and research for the American Public Power Association, had written a series of articles in *Public Power* magazine in which he laid out an economic justification for abandoning a decades-long practice of setting utility rates by linking customers to capital investment costs.

Electric utilities, he argued, need to set rates in the same manner as airlines or hotels. Just as hotels offer deeply discounted rates during the off season or airlines offer last-minute bargains for empty seats on flights, utilities should likewise offer deep discounts during off-peak periods to find ways to sell surplus power and charge high rates during periods when production facilities are in high demand.

The concept of allowing electricity prices to fluctuate with demand seems simple, but to veterans of utility rate design, it is heretical. Following publication of each of the articles in 2004, Kelly's phone rang often. Some callers argued for the status quo, while others, intrigued by Kelly's arguments, wanted to discuss the practical obstacles to implementing a new approach to costing and pricing electricity.

The phone calls and e-mails led to formation of an industry working group of rate specialists from nine utilities that met twice in 2005 to discuss practical aspects of moving to marginal cost pricing of electricity. Todd Hall, vice president of consumer services for Lincoln Electric System in Nebraska, telephoned Kelly to say the articles had sparked spirited debates among his rate staff and the utility would request funds for its 2005 budget to examine the impact of applying marginal cost concepts to electricity pricing.

Today, the once heretical notion of marginal cost pricing is increasingly accepted as analysts in utilities around the country stop arguing about whether they should even consider it and instead look for ways to make it happen.

How the Industry Got to This Point

Determining a price for a unit of electricity has, for decades, been a tortured process. Retail electricity prices are regulated either by state or local authorities and utility personnel cannot simply slap an arbitrary price on the product. Although there have been some notorious experiments over the years to give customers a choice of electricity prices, it is still a single utility whose wires feed into a home or business. Customers are buying electricity from a monopoly supplier.

Because of this monopoly status, government regulators insist that utilities demonstrate how much it costs them to serve their customers, then it must charge each group of customers (residential, small commercial, large commercial, industrial) a rate based on the cost of providing that service. When the utility is a stockholder-owned company, regulators allow a return on investment. Utilities operated by a municipality or other government entity charge enough to recover their investment in electric production and distribution facilities, but do not add on a profit.

Public Power

www.appanet.org/newsletters/ppmagazine.cfm

Established: 1942

Publisher: American Public Power Association, Washington, D.C.

Frequency: Bimonthly

Characteristics: Four color, average 60 pages

Circulation: 20,000, controlled subscription

Readership: U.S. municipal power officials

Editorial staff: Editor, art director, three contributing editors

Determining how much to charge each group of customers is a complex undertaking for electric utilities. If the utility, for example, pays $300 million to build a generating facility, it must recover this capital investment plus operating expenses from its various customer groups. Operating expenses, such as fuel costs, can be readily assigned to customers, but assigning the costs of capital investments used to serve them is much less clear.

In his series of articles calling for an industry move away from this allocation process, Kelly argued that the overhead capital costs and operating costs of the multi-million dollar generating plants used to produce electricity should be recovered by a structure of prices that reflect the marginal cost of producing electricity at various times. These costs can range from just a few cents to 15 cents or more, depending on the highest cost plant used at a particular time.

The major benefit of marginal cost pricing is that it would significantly increase the use of existing generation facilities and at the same time reduce demand during peak times. This increased usage results in more kilowatt-hours being spread over less capacity, and consumers—as long as prices reflect marginal costs—pay lower rates on average.

Thanks to the Kelly articles, the industry was having a much-needed debate over pricing reform, but for many executives, institutional resistance to change remained a formidable hurdle. Even Mike McMahon, whose fable did much to breathe life into the debate, was skeptical about practicalities of migrating from cost-of-service allocation to marginal cost pricing.

The economic arguments are valid, he said. But electricity prices charged by Snohomish County Public Utility District must be approved by a three-member elected board of directors. Whenever you change rate design, you're going to have winners and losers. "Even if overall rates are going down, some people's bills may actually go up. How do you make a change that isn't so dramatic so people's bills won't change in dramatic ways?"

Some rate experts in the industry are eager to move to marginal cost pricing of electricity. One of them is Tim Miller, senior rate analyst for Missouri River Energy Services, a power supply agency headquartered in Sioux Falls, S.D. In the jargon of the municipal electric utility business, Missouri River Energy Services is a "joint action agency" that is owned by several utilities and provides power to them. Despite the hurdles, inadequate electricity supplies might trigger a more industry-wide embrace of marginal cost pricing of electricity, Miller said. He equates it to gasoline prices. If gas stations artificially kept fuel prices at $3 a gallon, even though it was costing them $4, consumers would buy too much gas because they would not have that price signal, he said.

The move to a more efficient pricing approach should logically start with large industrial customers, which might account for half of a utility's total kilowatt-hour sales, Miller said.

One utility that has made that move is IID Energy in Imperial, Calif., which introduced time-of-use rates in 2006. Electricity prices vary between winter and summer and over the course of each day, said Bob Fugett, general superintendent for energy services. The utility's prices will be highest during the peak demand hours of 11 a.m. to 7 p.m. each day and lowest during overnight hours.

Because of the nature of the utility industry, change comes at a glacial pace. With word on marginal pricing now out, some form of shift industry-wide is no longer an academic idea; it's an idea the industry is taking seriously.

—*Jeanne LaBella*

What 'Cost' Means ... and the Cost of Not Knowing

By John Kelly

Nothing is more common, it's been said, than for people to think that because they are familiar with words, they understand the ideas they stand for. A popular rendition of this observation is that it's not the things you don't know that get you in trouble but the things you know that aren't true. Both sayings can be aptly applied to popular conceptions of the term "cost."

The dictionary defines cost as the amount of money asked or paid for a thing. This definition is often good enough. It's a serviceable one when discussing the cost of a meal in a restaurant, vegetables in a grocery store, or tickets to a ball game. But the definition quickly becomes inadequate when the determination of cost involves durable goods, such as capital investments. Even determining the cost of relatively basic, consumer durable goods such as an automobile or computer printer becomes more complicated. The respective operating costs of gasoline and cartridge refills will affect the total costs of these goods. Likewise, in the simplest industrial setting (in terms of cost determination) where a firm produces only one product and the capital investment used to produce it is totally devoted to that product, the "cost," usually thought of as "average cost," will vary. It will vary as the output, the productive life of a capital investment, and the investment's eventual salvage value vary. The determination of average cost becomes even less manageable when the investment is a large piece of capital equipment used to produce or supply more than one product or service, oftentimes numerous ones.

There is nothing new regarding the difficulties of arriving at a meaningful definition of cost for business decision-making. These difficulties exist in utility and non-utility industries alike. But in the utility sector — to put the best face on things — they are unknown, forgotten, avoided, or misunderstood. In the worst case, they are swept under the carpet or used to promote price discrimination or cross-class subsidies. Traditional methods for costing electric service produce significantly different, and sometimes mathematically contradictory, estimates. Because tens of millions of dollars are usually at stake, and because differing cost estimates result in significant differences in prices, it would seem that the fundamental reasons for the inconsistencies would be more closely scrutinized. Usually they aren't.

Instead, they are ignored or glibly dismissed with a statement that cost allocation is an art rather than a science. But such reactions are more indicative of a lack of a sound conceptual understanding of the nature of relevant costs rather than suggesting a need for experience and judgment in estimating costs.

It is common to read or hear statements that it is imperative to know the real cost of electricity. The statements seldom come, however, with a clear definition of what "real" cost means, how to estimate it, or its implications. One exception is the demand in recent years for a return to cost-based rates after federal and state deregulation adventures resulted in gross abuses of market power that drove prices to levels that exceeded almost anyone's definition of reasonable cost. The cost-based rates demanded were those that reflect traditional notions of real costs. Though estimates based on traditional methods may serve as a rough benchmark to gauge the magnitude of gross abuses of market power, they are inadequate as an indicator of the true cost of electricity, or for the efficient, day-to-day operation of electric power generating facilities.

The central feature of traditional costing methodologies is the estimation of demand charges. These charges are attempts to allocate portions of capital expenditures for generating capacity to particular customer classes, or in some cases to individual, large customers. The charges are supposed to indicate the relative amounts of existing generating capacity customers are responsible for, and are intended to compensate utilities for having capacity available to meet the demand for electric service.

Traditional allocation methods seem reasonable enough on the surface, and this may be why the serious problems underlying them are not confronted. But estimates of demand charges are based on any one of an a la carte menu of coincident and non-coincident peak factors. The choice of which to use is arbitrary since there are no fixed rules for choosing; it is left to the costing practitioner's judgment. This would not necessarily be harmful if the different coincident and non-coincident methods produced similar estimates of real cost. But they don't. Rather, they result in significantly different estimates of the prices that various customer groups should pay.

Demand charge calculations attempt to do the impossible: allocate the common costs of generating facilities in an economically meaningful way. The questionable logic of demand charge calculations is obvious when it is applied to a large-city hotel that caters to business travelers. During peak seasons, rooms may rent for $200 per night; but during non-peak times, they may let for $100. An individual who books a room during peak season does not have to pay the same $200 rate if he or she returns during non-peak season. The hotel does not — cannot in the face of competition, and will not when faced with an oversupply of rooms — collect a demand charge from non-peak customers simply because they may have stayed at the hotel during a peak period. Though hotel and electric power industries are much different, they are similar to the extent that both require relatively large amounts of capital investment, and the nature of these costs are "common." The costs cannot be traced home and attributed to particular electricity services in the same direct and obvious way in which, as economist John Maurice Clark puts it, leather can be traced to the shoes that are made from it. An increase or decrease in output of electric services does not involve a proportionate increase or decrease in cost.

There is always the necessity, of course, to recover common capital investment costs, but there is an important difference in the way the hotel industry and electric power industry go about this task. Electric utilities rely on accounting conventions that are manifested in demand charges, which are largely due to historic accident. Hotels, on the other hand, rely on an understanding of cost that reflects the economic reality of doing business in markets with significant competitive pressures. They focus on the actual impact of decisions on net income. The different approaches have important implications for how efficiently existing facilities are used in the respective industries.

Despite their readily apparent and serious shortcomings, cost-based methodologies continue to occupy center stage. Decades of repetition have reinforced the belief that the methodologies associated with the term cost-based rates do, in fact, measure real costs. Another reason why traditional costing methods have endured is because they have been protected from serious scrutiny due to the monopoly environments in which utilities typically operate. In contradiction to the belief that such methodologies measure the true cost of electric service is the fact that their very shortcomings are the major impetus behind many so-called "innovative" rate and demand-side management programs aimed at shaving peak loads (as opposed to programs aimed at general or long-run decreases in demand). If prices reflected the true costs of electricity in the first place, it is difficult to see why such programs would be necessary.

Understanding the real cost of electricity requires understanding a few, selected economic concepts. Too often, any discussion of these concepts is quickly dismissed as abstract or impractical. The old saw is heard: "True in theory but wrong in practice." But, it has been aptly said that what is true in theory is also true in practice, or else something was wrong with the theory in the first place. Dismissive statements about theory sidestep basic questions about the economic facts and a realistic understanding of how they hang together.

Ironically, traditional costing approaches themselves rest on several unrealistic assumptions. One is that capital investments in generating facilities are not subject to market forces of supply and demand. It is assumed that the supply of, and demand for, electric generating services will be such that costs, prices and utilization will vary little from what was originally forecast when a plant was built. Such a view is analogous to a hotel pricing policy that locks room prices into a formula based on the original capital costs incurred, the rate of return desired when the hotel was built, and a desire for a particular stream of future payments to recover investment costs. One result of such pricing inflexibility is an underutilization of facilities accompanied by a significant loss of revenues both when the demand is higher or lower than originally anticipated. More serious is the assumption, already mentioned, that common or overhead costs can be allocated to services or customers in an economically meaningful way. The investment expenditures for most electric generating facilities fall into the category of a common cost, which cannot be traced directly to each 8,760 hours of the year, or to customers, for that matter. Though this basic economic fact of life is widely known and well documented, it goes widely unheeded. It seems to become confused with special cases in which facilities are dedicated to particular customers and, at the same time, there is also a high probability that the dedicated facilities will, in fact, be paid for by those customers. Capital investments in these situations would not qualify as common costs.

The economic view of real cost is simpler and more direct. Better yet, it is more instinctive than the traditional view. It is based on the notion of opportunity costs, which says the true cost of any action can be measured by the value of the best alternative that must be foregone when the action is taken. More specifically, in a business context, economist Ronald Coase defines costs as "the [net] receipts that would have been obtained if [a] particular decision had not been taken." This view of cost recognizes that not all past business expenditures and expenses are relevant for every pricing decision. Relevant costs are those that actually affect net income. They are incremental or avoidable costs rather than averaged or sunk costs, and they do not include allocated portions of common costs.

Commenting on the costing and pricing of electric services almost 50 years ago, highly regarded economist William Vickrey observed: "The dominant issue is one of whether the pattern of [electric] rates should be based on tradition, inertia, and happenstance, or whether it is to be developed by careful weighing of the relevant factors with a view of guiding consumers to make efficient use of facilities that are available."

During the missteps and fiascos of utility industry deregulation efforts over the past decade, very important economic principles have been ignored or twisted: one is the crucial issue of the pattern of electric rates — a pattern of rates that reflect real cost of electricity. Instead of keeping focused on this central issue, deregulation advocates have been preoccupied with questionable hopes and ideological beliefs that electric power markets are, or can be, effectively competitive. The debate over the relative competitiveness of electric power markets is likely to continue for many years. Nevertheless, during this time and under current forms of economic regulation (i.e., federal and state rate regulation of private utilities, and public ownership of state and local utilities) important changes can be made in the pattern of rates that would significantly increase capacity utilization and, consequently, effect lower rates. One major impediment to this happening is the lack of a proper and clear understanding of what cost really means. Other factors are inertia and a lack of political will to initiate change.

Public power utilities in the United States have done an exemplary job over the decades in providing electric service at rates free of monopoly profit and significantly below those of regulated private utilities. At the same time, they have provided superior service because they are community-owned and operated. In this important regard, they have been efficient because revenues reflected prudently incurred expenditures and expenses. Local political control reinforced the economic and personal motivations of managers to operate efficiently. But on a less apparent — yet very important — level, there are significant opportunities to increase efficiency and reduce rates by using existing generating facilities more efficiently. More efficient patterns of electric rates would increase capacity factors and spread the common costs of generating facilities over more kilowatt-hours sold. At the same time, it would reduce the amount of capacity required to meet peak demands.

Reproduced with permission from the American Public Power Association.

JOURNALISM
THAT
MATTERS

Chapter 19

Turning a Club Into a Rock Star

An innovative nightclub gets a boost when a Nightclub & Bar
writer recognizes the significance of the club's ideas

Matthew Bongiovi, ultra-lounge principal and brother of famous rocker Jon Bon Jovi, once told me in a Las Vegas nightclub, "You guys are the *Rolling Stone* of the industry."

He was referring to the trade magazine I edit, *Nightclub & Bar,* and while I wouldn't presume to put too much stock in Bongiovi's remark, I can certainly say the magazine carries a lot of weight with the club owners and managers we count among our readers. I can also say that, in some cases, the magazine plays a pivotal role in whether, or how well, a club concept takes off in our industry.

Rockstar Destin in Destin, Fla., is one club whose success as a nightspot concept traveled quickly throughout the industry and, at the end of 2005, landed the owner onto the agenda of the industry's main national conference as a result of our coverage.

We don't ordinarily profile new clubs for the simple reason that many of them, if their concept doesn't take hold, can't be counted on to make it past their first lease payment. For that reason, we like to see at least a six-month financial and operational track record before we consider writing a profile. But in this case we took a chance. Based on experience with what business plans succeed in the long run and our gut feeling, we gave our associate editor Jenny Adams the okay to break our rule—and the result was a phenomenal success for us and the club.

Adams learned about the club while in Las Vegas for the industry's show, called the Nightclub & Bar Beverage Retailer, Beverage and Food Convention Trade Show. People in the industry know it as "The Show" because of its centrality for industry networking, and when Adams was there, her networking paid off. While taking a coffee break in the Las Vegas Hilton, Jay Bartoline sidled up to do the same and the two got to talking about Bartoline's latest project. He had been named general manger of a club that was set to open in another month and, as Adams puts it, his excitement about the difference of this club concept was unusually high. "You would have thought he was building this place from the ground up with his bare hands," she says.

After 45 minutes of talking, Adams knew she had a hot story on her hands, and a few months later, after first running a short news item about the club opening, she was on the phone to Bartoline and the club's 28-year-old owner, Rik Bos, for lengthy interviews to get at the heart of what made the club different. She also interviewed the bar manager and one of the executives of the company who was providing the financial backing. Karim Shamsi-Basha, a top flight photographer with credits in *People* and other consumer and business magazines, was sent to Destin to put into pictures the excitement Bartoline had conveyed to Adams in their first meeting.

"All the money, disco balls, and DJ prowess in the world won't add up to a successful club," says Adams, "but after speaking with Jay, I could see the club's advantages from his perspective instantly. Combined with Rik Bos' sheer passion for the project, a successful outcome was virtually inevitable."

Not Another Tiki Hut

The club was a totally new approach to the local market, where most nightspots are casual, catering to the T-shirt and shorts crowd out looking for half-priced beer and a bucket of oysters. But Bos believed young beachcombers were ready to dress up for a night of high-energy, New York-style dancing. What's more, Bos had the financial backing to start the club off right and the track record to keep it running strong. He cut his teeth running two largely successful Florida clubs.

Inside and out, Rockstar was designed to be elite, mysterious, beautiful, and sexy. Preparing club patrons for the sell is necessary in all business, but for this project, Bos needed to convince the party crowd there was a definite reason to toss the Tevas and slip on the stilettos. He accomplished it through attention to detail in every corner of customer service.

Nightclub&Bar

For the On Premise Innovator

Nightclub & Bar

www.nightclub.com

Established: 1985

Publisher: Oxford Publishing, Oxford, Miss.

Frequency: Monthly

Characteristics: Four-color, average 86 pages

Circulation: 35,000 companies

Readership: Nightclub owners and managers

Editorial staff: Editor, associate editor, contributing editor, 3 in-house writers, two in-house designers, and freelance production workers

The club was built on the waterside, in an old bar for fisherman known as the Hurricane Hole. Bos rehabbed the 30-year-old building and linked it to a floating barge nearby, creating a smoking space outside the main room and adding a unique element of style. Swaying slightly with the evening tides, the barge has enough space for 250 people to take in the night air or enjoy a fine cigar.

Inside, Bos installed overhead laser lights, lined the walls with plush seating, and had servers prepare high-end cuts of steak on oven-heated slabs of granite tableside. "Everything was designed with an eye toward pulling in females looking for a place to party not for a few hours but all night long," says Adams. "Where the girls are, the guys will follow. It makes perfect sense, but to our knowledge, no one in Destin had tried this concept before."

Our coverage made the club's early weeks a much bigger success than what it would have been. Right off the bat the club was taking in $3,500 in bottle service and more than $17,000 in total till on a typical Saturday night, far higher than a club expects to take in so soon after launch.

Local people in the industry, after reading the profile, had to check the place out for themselves and are now trying out some of his ideas, changing the way people in Destin party. "I got feedback from people who worked in the industry and who read the story and came because of it," says Bos. "It was a great success for us."

Bos used the release of our August issue, which featured Rockstar Destin on the cover, as a promotional event, piquing the interest of area club patrons and boosting business. Probably more importantly, though, the coverage set the stage for his team and clientele to know they were on the ground floor of a very promising project. "Having the notoriety [of the magazine coverage did] more for business," Bos says. "It gave the staff a sense of accomplishment, and ultimately it will give us more credibility as one of the best nightclubs in the country that people will hear about."

What's more, it gave Bos national exposure within the club industry, including publicity at the industry's principal annual trade show in Las Vegas, which *Nightclub & Bar* sponsors. It also is showing that New York-style clubs can turn a T-shirt kind of place like Destin upside down.

—*Taylor Rau*

Editor's Note: The club has since changed its name to Jet Ultra Lounge.

Party Like Rockstar

Destin, Fla.'s Catchy Concept is a Seaside Success

By Jenny Adams

Sending a wave of excitement through Destin, Fla.'s nightlife market, Rockstar Destin is spelling big profits for one of America's youngest clubs. Destin's stretch of pristine white sand makes Florida's aptly named Emerald Coast a destination for tens of thousands each year, and for the last decade, the small beach community has been a place to kick off shoes and relax, sans make-up or a tie, over a half-priced beer and bucket of local oysters.

One man, however, one very young man at that, has seen Destin through a different pair of rose-tinted sunglasses. Instead of viewing the market as eternally low-key and easy-going, he is placing a bet on women donning their little black dresses and the men suiting up for a high-energy, upscale night out on the town. Far away from the reverberating club beats of New York and Los Angeles, there suddenly is a very viable market for the newly shining Rockstar Destin, and Florida's late-night connoisseur is falling in love.

Visionary Vitality

Rik Bos, at 28 years old, knows what he is doing in the restaurant and bar industry. "I was fortunate," he says of his late success.

"I had a track record." That track record includes ownership of Blues and Harry T's, both previously successful in the Florida nightlife scene, under the parent corporation of Legendary Entertainment Inc. However, Bos, and Legendary, went out on a totally new limb in May of 2005, by opening Rockstar Destin, the resort town's first and only high-energy dance club.

Stepping across the threshold, patrons are met by two hostesses clad in tall black boots and wearing friendly smiles against a backdrop of visual prowess. Tables flank the left side and, with a bar to the right of the first DJ booth, as well as one in the back, the place screams, "Grab a cocktail and a seat — it is going to be a long night." The VIP room, constructed from what was originally an old dock, now taunts boat captains idling out to sea with a glimpse of the good life through the spotless glass windows.

The voice and visuals of Rockstar Destin are provided by some of the top leaders in the industry, and guests are treated to a sensual experience every evening on the dance floor, as well as in the VIP room. Selected and installed by Bos' longtime Harry T's DJ, DJ D.P., the sound setup includes a Pioneer DJM 600 mixer and two Pioneer CDJ 1000s. "We use Martin throughout," Bos says. "Honestly, there is no light room like it. The light crystals are amazing to watch."

The group unleashed the club concept onto the virgin beach scene, and with the promotions going strong, the lineup includes DJ Epheny taking the booth at 9 p.m., mixing an eclectic lounge vibe every night, followed by The Chris McCarty band, playing live on stage for only one set from 10:30 to 11:30, Thursday through Saturday.

"I want people to drink earlier," Bos explains. "It creates a fill because people need to get in and watch the one set. It is also incentive for the band to play well, and then they are done and they become part of the experience."

The experience definitely continues as midnight strikes — with Rockstar in full swing as DJ D.P. mixes popular Hip-Hop and House beats, complemented by VIP amenities rarely found outside a metropolitan hub. The average cover charge is around $20, but ladies are always ushered in free.

Securing a seat in the plush VIP section, making it a truly extravagant evening, costs nothing to reserve, but might run up to

$200 for the required minimum depending on the date. The beauty of the VIP treatment here, however, is that reserving a table negates the cover charge for each person in the party.

"Any time you go out to a bar and you see tables and there are people sitting there and they are not drinking, they are just taking up a table for people that want to sit and drink and spend money. So if you want to sit down, we don't charge you for the table," says Julie Cotton, vp of marketing for Legendary Inc. "It's just the minimum. We designed that so people can come in and get a table if they plan on really partying. If they buy the bottle, it pretty much covers the table minimum. We haven't had any issue with someone not meeting their table minimum, they usually go way over."

With the ability to serve around 400 guests, inside and out, Rockstar's initial sales reports are sizzling. A Saturday night will bring in around $3,500 in bottle service and more than $17,000 for the total till. With construction costs just north of $800,000, the club is thriving in its fledgling months and fated to be Destin's new after-hours destination.

Rough Seas

Rockstar's inception was not a golden road from the onset, however. Destin has never known a serious New York-style nightlife scene, and the question for Bos and his crew was, "Does the town want and need one?"

Finding the right locale was the first crucial hurdle in the process, and Bos admits that it has partly supplied the instant success. "The bar was an existing building that was probably more than 30 years old," he says.

Before Rockstar was ever a diva, she was known to locals as The Hurricane Hole, a place frequented by 10 to 15 fisherman at a time after a long day on the job. "It had a concrete bar, and people were typically drinking whiskey," Bos says. "It was a pretty wild environment six months ago."

For many locals, the idea of a mega-club is far more outrageous. Bos hired architect Bill Pope for the exterior, and designer Susan Boyd, acclaimed for her work on the Del Frisco in Las Vegas, to add the striking style of the inside.

"If you were going to do this building today, you'd never be able to get it done because of the way the codes are written out," Bos says.

Destin's laws now place heavy restrictions on new construction extending out over the water due to hurricane damage and land preservation. "That's where this building is so unique. It gave me an opportunity to actually build a nightclub on the water."

The attached floating barge adds the necessary smoking space outside as well as one more element of style. Swaying slightly with the evening tides, there is enough space for another 250 guests to enjoy a cigarette or fine cigar and the breathtaking view of the Destin Pass.

Late at night, DJ Epheny moves outside to become the mistress of a totally separate booth, spinning beats to ensure the party never slows. "This is the first kind of upscale place for a younger clientele to come," Cotton says. "I would say the reason they come is partly because of our location."

Preparing for the Upscale

Inside and out, Rockstar was designed to be elite, mysterious, beautiful and sexy. Preparing them for the up sell is necessary in almost all business, but in this endeavor, Bos needed to convince the patrons there was a definite reason to toss the Tevas and slip on the stilettos. He accomplished it through attention to detail in every corner of customer service.

The name Rockstar actually is a sort of Siamese symbolism. Of course, everyone is treated like a celebrity within the walls, but the other motive for the appellation was the unique "Hot Rock" style of the food presentation. Executive Chef Billy Ballou prepares fresh ingredients nightly, centering around three main choices of entrée, including freshly caught yellow fin tuna, shrimp and a center-cut filet mignon, each accompanied by an array of steamed vegetables and signature dipping sauces.

Large slabs of granite rock, heated for more than 12 hours in a special-purpose oven, are set on the table with the rare food spread on top. At around 400 degrees each, the granite rocks supply an instant dry heat release, searing the food, while confining the natural juices inside. Similar to the allure of the Japanese hibachi, patrons can enjoy a more interactive, exciting dinner.

Drowning in Drink Sales

The drinks also adhere to a high level of quality, from the fresh fruit to the extreme premium selection. Bar Manager Melinda Burger has 10 years experience in the industry, and prepared more than 60 drinks, prior to opening night, for the upper-level staff to taste when deciding on the signature drink list. "It was a several-day process," she says.

Two of the main choices that found residency on the list include the Wokka Saké, a mixture of vodka and saké infused with passion fruit, and the Rockstar, containing vodka, Southern Comfort, peach schnapps, amaretto, pineapple, orange and grenadine. This attention to detail doesn't even raise the cost across the bar in Rockstar Destin — it comes standard for every patron.

"We keep the pricing reasonable," Burger says. "We love our locals, and this is such a great bar that we want people to feel dressed up and special when they come in." Ensuring the sparkling service is a staff of eight servers and five bartenders, 80 percent of whom have worked in one of Bos' previous Destin ventures.

"That was what really gave me the confidence to do it ... that we had such a great team," Bos says. "I was fortunate — the core bartenders and core doormen are all the same."

Reproduced with permission from Oxford Publishing.

About the Contributors

John Gannon, "Coming Clean on Bad Chemical Data," page 41. Gannon is senior editor, *Right-to-Know Planning Guide*, Bureau of National Affairs, Washington, D.C.

Sherry L. Harowitz, "Better Ideas, Better Security," page 183. Harowitz is editor-in-chief, *Security Management*, ASIS International, Alexandria, Va.

Catherine A. Kreyche, "Saying Hello to the Elephant in the Room," page 127. Kreyche is a communication strategist with Management Concepts, Vienna, Va.

Jeanne LaBella, "Rattling the Electricity Pricing Cage," page 193. LaBella is editor, *Public Power*, and vice president, American Public Power Association, Washington, D.C.

Alice Lipowicz, "Caught in a Feedback Loop," page 111. Lipowicz is a reporter for *Washington Technology*, Post Newsweek Tech Media, Washington, D.C.

Michael Martin, "Switching the Current on Electrical Rebates," page 121. Martin is editor, *The Electrical Distributor*, National Association of Electrical Distributors, St. Louis, Mo.

Molly Moses, "When U.S.-Canada Tax Relations Hang in the Balance," page 94. Moses is editor/reporter, *Transfer Pricing Report*, Bureau of National Affairs, Washington, D.C.

Taylor Rau, "Turning a Club into a Rock Star," page 204. Rau is editor, *Nightclub & Bar*, Oxford Publishing, Oxford, Miss.

Matthew Rushton, "Judging the Judges," page 55. Rushton is a contributor to *Legal Business*, Legalease, London.

Claire Sandt Chiamulera, "Raising a Legal Bar to Improve Children's Lives," page 166. Sandt-Chiamulera is editor-in-chief, *ABA Child Law Practice*, ABA Center on Children and the Law, Washington, D.C.

Beatrice Schriever, "Sounding the Alarm on the Teacher Shortage," page 150. Schriever is a contributor to *Professionally Speaking*, Ontario College of Teachers, Toronto.

David Silverberg, "Trauma Care on Life Support," page 136. Silverberg is editor, *HSToday*, KMD Media LLC, McLean, Va.

Frank Tiboni, "Getting Real on Virtual Espionage," page 28. Tiboni is a former senior editor at *Federal Computer Week*, FCW Media Group, Falls Church, Va.

Katy Tomasulo, "Second Thoughts on a Lobbying Plan," page 81. Tomasulo is managing editor, *Prosales and Tools of the Trade*, Hanley-Wood, Washington, D.C.

Michelle Vanderhoff, "Off the Critical Path," page 70. Vanderhoff is editor and project manager at the American Physical Therapy Association, Alexandria, Va.

Patience Wait, "Not Worth the Paper It's Printed On," page 88. Wait is a senior writer at *Government Computer News*, Post Newsweek Tech Media, Washington, D.C.

Christopher M. Wright, "Taking the Specter Out of 'Spec Abuse'," page 158. Wright is a freelance writer in Washington, D.C., specializing in business and investment topics for U.S. and international clients.

About the Editors

Robert Freedman is senior editor, *Realtor*® *Magazine*, National Association of Realtors®, Washington, D.C., and the 2003-2005 president of the American Society of Business Publication Editors. Freedman is editor of *Best Practices of the Business Press* (Kendall-Hunt, 2003), a compilation of essays on B2B publication editing, and *Broker to Broker: Lessons from America's Most Successful Real Estate Brokerages* (John Wiley & Sons, 2005), a compilation of management tactics first published in *Realtor*® *Magazine*.

Steven Roll is state tax law editor, *State Tax Report*, Bureau of National Affairs, Washington, D.C., and president of the Washington, D.C., chapter of the American Society of Business Publication Editors. Roll, an adjunct instructor of business law at Strayer University, has a law degree from the University of Baltimore School of Law and has written for *Business Week Online*, among other business publications.

Index

Other Important Books for
Business Journalists
From Marion Street Press, Inc.

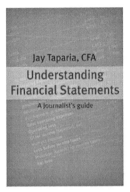

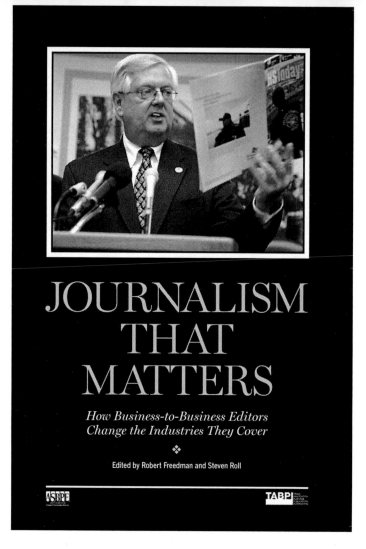

Spread the word!

Quantity discounts are available for
Journalism That Matters. Let everyone on your staff
have a copy of this inspiring book.

10 to 19 copies = 10 percent discount
20 to 49 copies = 20 percent discount
50+ copies = 30 percent discount

Call Ed Avis to order, 866-443-7987
edavis@marionstreetpress.com